The Believer's New Life

Andrew Murray

BETHANY HOUSE PUBLISHERS
MINNEAPOLIS, MINNESOTA 55438
A Division of Bethany Fellowship, Inc.

Translated from the Dutch by Rev. J. P. Lilley, M.A., and previously published under the title *The New Life*.

This edition has been newly edited.

Printed in the United States of America

Library of Congress Cataloging in Publication Data

Murray, Andrew, 1828–1917.
  The believer's new life.

  (The Andrew Murray Christian maturity library)
    1. Christian life—1960–   I. Title.   II. Series.
BV4501.2.M86 1984   248.4   83–3006
ISBN 0–87123–431–9 (pbk.)

Translator's Note

A glance at the pages of this book will show that it is more basic than the other writings of its honored author. The reason is that it is specifically designed for young disciples who need nothing so much as to sit at the feet of Jesus and hear His Word.

Every minister of a congregation in which young people have been brought to the Lord will remember the anxiety that swept over his heart as he contemplated their entrance on the duties and responsibilities of a public Christian confession. The supreme question at such a time is: How will these young believers be built up in the knowledge of the truth? How can they best be taught the real nature of the new life they have received, the dangers by which it is surrounded, and the directions in which its energy may safely go forth?

The desire to give a suitable answer to these questions has given rise to many excellent manuals. Especially in connection with times of revival, new books for this circle of readers always make their appearance. As Mr. Murray indicates in the Preface, it was in the midst of such a happy period that the following chapters were written.

The volume came under my notice while I was recently traveling in Holland. A brief inspection showed me that it was one of the most simple and comprehensive of its class. Now translated into English from the latest Dutch edition, the many thousands who have profited by Mr. Murray's other admirable works have a suitable book to give or recommend to those who are setting their faces toward an earnest and fruitful Christian life.

That it will be very helpful to this end I cannot doubt—especially if the directions the author himself has given are faithfully adhered to. The chapters are comparatively short and include a considerable number of Bible references. The reader is encouraged to turn to and examine the texts marked. This practice, if persistently carried out, cannot fail to yield a rich harvest. It might be noted that there are just as many chapters in the book as Sabbaths in the year. Thus, another use of the book could be within a family devotional setting—reading one chapter each week and then discussing it as a family.

I have only to add that the volume is now translated and issued with Mr. Murray's cordial sanction. It has been to me a very pleasant task to put it into English for my younger brethren throughout the country. Beyond this point, of course, my responsibility does not go. Should the book prove useful in guiding yet further in the way of peace and holiness the feet of those who have come to the Lord, it will be, both for author and translator, the answer to many a fervent prayer.

J. P. Lilley
Arbroath,
September 1891

Preface

In talking with new believers, I have frequently longed for a suitable book in which the most important truths concerning the *new life* were briefly and simply set forth. I could not find anything that entirely corresponded with what I desired. Since Whitsuntide, 1884, I have taken part in services in which I have spoken with many who professed to have found the Lord but who were, nevertheless, still very weak in knowledge and faith, and this need was felt by me still more keenly. In the course of my journey, I felt pressed to begin to write.

I was under a vivid impression of the distortions and the perverted thoughts concerning the new life with which, as was manifest from conversations with them, almost all young Christians have to wrestle. I wished, through some words of instruction and encouragement, to help them see what a glorious life of power and joy is prepared for them in their Lord Jesus, and how simple is the way to enjoy all this blessing.

I have confined myself in these writings to the most important topics of the new life. First there is *the Word of God* as the glorious and trustworthy guide, even for the simplest believers who will only surrender themselves to it. Second, *the Son, the gift of the Father*, as the chief element in the Word, to do all for us. Third, what the Scriptures teach concerning *sin*, as that which we must bring to Jesus and from which He will set us free.

Fourth, there is *faith*, the word, which expresses our inability to bring or do anything to earn salvation. It must be received every day of our life as a gift from above. Fifth, *the Holy Spirit,* with whom the young Christian must make his acquaintance, as the person through whom the Word and Jesus, with all His work and through faith in Him, can become power and truth. Sixth, *the holy life* of obedience and of fruitfulness in which the Spirit teaches us to walk.

It is to these six basic thoughts of the new life that I have confined myself, with the ceaseless prayer that God may use what I have written to help new believers understand what a glorious and mighty life they have received from their Father.

It was often with great hesitation that I parted company with the new believers who had to go back to lonely places, where they would have little counsel or help and would seldom fellowship in the true preaching of the Word. It is my sure and confident expectation that what the Lord has given me to write will prove an aid to many of these young confessors.

While writing this book, I have had a second wish for the reader. I have wondered what I could possibly do to make certain that my writing would not draw away attention from the Word of God, but rather help to make the Word more precious. I resolved to provide the reader with footnote references so that on every major point that was dealt with, the reader might be stirred to listen *to the Word itself, to God himself.*

I am hopeful that this arrangement will yield a double benefit. Many do not know and have no one to teach them how to examine the Scriptures properly. If the reader will meditate on each point and then look up the texts that are quoted, he will begin to learn how to consult God's Word when he wants to understand a teaching. The book may also be of use for study in weekly prayer meetings or social gatherings for the study of the Word. If used in these settings, each member should read the assigned chapter and review the texts that seem to him the most important. The leader of the meeting may then read the portion aloud and open it up for discussion.

In our congregation we have found that the benefit of this type of meeting is very great. This practice leads to the searching of God's Word in a way that preaching does not. It stirs the members of the congregation, especially the young people, to independent dealing with the Word. It leads to a more living fellowship among the members of Christ's body, and that leads to an upbuilding in love. It prepares the way for a recognition of the Word as the living communication of the thoughts of God, with which divine power will work that which is pleasing to God.

I am persuaded that there are many believing men and women asking what they can accomplish for the Lord. With this type of study and discussion they could become the channels of great blessing. Let them meet once a week with some of their neighbors or friends to hear texts read which they have all been previously studying. The Lord will certainly give His blessing to such a gathering.

I would request one thing more of the reader. Try reading every portion over at least three times. The great shortcoming of all our searchings into the divine things is superficiality. When we read anything and understand it somewhat, we think that this is enough. No! we must give *time*, that it may make an impression and wield its own influence upon us.

Read every portion *the first time with consideration*, to understand the good that is in it; and then see if you receive benefit from the thoughts that are expressed. Read it *the second time to see if it is really in accordance with God's Word*. Take some, if not all, of the verses that are presented on each point, and ponder them in order to come under the full force of what God has said on the issue. Let your God, through His Word, teach you what you must think and believe concerning Him and His will. Read it then *the third time to find out how it relates to your own life* in order to know if your life has been in harmony with the new life, and to direct your life for the future entirely according to God's Word. I am fully persuaded that the time spent with the Word of God will be rewarded tenfold.

I pray that the Lord may confirm His work in you. I have not become weary of crying to you; the blessedness and the power of the new life that is in you are greater than you know. Only learn to trust in Jesus, the gift of God, and to know correctly the Scriptures, the Word of God. Only give Him time to hold conversation with you and to work in you, and your heart shall overflow with the blessedness of God.

Now to Him who is able to do more than exceedingly above all that we ask or think, to Him be glory in the Church to all eternity.

Andrew Murray
Wellington, South Africa
August 12, 1885

Contents

Introduction to the 1984 Edition

Some years ago, I was trying to decide which were the most important biblical truths to teach the high school girls who came to my apartment every Tuesday night. Many of them were new Christians and some of them had grown up with very little church background. Then I heard my pastor remark that in his opinion *New Life in Christ* by Andrew Murray was the best book to use with new Christians. I bought a copy and was thrilled and blessed by the things I read. In this book I found compassionate understanding of the weakness felt by new Christians, blended with a no-compromise stand on the total surrender of one's life to Christ. The strength and love of Jesus which make obedience to God possible were clearly set forth.

However, I realized that this was a book which could be given only to a person already familiar with Old English expressions and church terminology. I had to carefully "translate" these lessons into language my students could understand. Many ideas from these lessons became part of my first book, *If God Loves Me, Why Can't I Get My Locker Open?*

How wonderful to have this marvelous Murray book now available in a readable, up-to-date form! I would highly recommend *The Believer's New Life* to both new Christians and those who have known Jesus for many years.

Lorraine Peterson

CHAPTER 1

The New Life

"For God so loved the world, that he gave his only begotten Son, that whosoever believeth in him should not perish, but have everlasting life" (John 3:16).

"For ye are dead, and your life is hid with Christ in God. . . . Christ . . . is our life" (Col. 3:3, 4).

"We . . . shew unto you that eternal life, which was with the Father, and was manifested unto us. . . . God hath given unto us eternal life, and this life is in his Son. He that hath the Son hath life" (1 John 1:2; 5:11, 12).

Glorious is the blessing which everyone receives who believes in the Lord Jesus. Not only does there come a change in his character and manner of life; he also receives from God out of heaven an entirely new life. He is born anew, born of God; he has passed from death into life.[1]

This new life is nothing less than eternal life.[2] This does not mean, as many think, that our life shall not end and endure into eternity. No, eternal life is nothing less than the very life of God, the life that He has had in himself from eternity and that has been visibly revealed in Christ. This life is now the gift to every child of God.[3]

This life is a life of inconceivable power. Whenever God gives life to a young plant or animal, that life has in itself the power of growth, whereby the plant or animal by itself

---

[1]John 1:12, 13; 3:5, 7; 5:24; 1 John 3:14; 5:1
[2]John 3:15, 16, 36; 6:40, 51; 11:25, 26; Rom. 6:11, 23; 8:2; 1 John 5:12, 13
[3]1 John 1:3; 3:1; 5:11

14

becomes large. Life is power. In the new life—that is, in your heart—there is the power of eternity.[4] More certain than the healthy growth of any tree or animal is the growth and maturing of the child of God who in reality surrenders himself to the working of the new life.

Basically, two things hinder this power and the reception of the new spiritual life. One is *ignorance of the nature of this life*—its laws and workings. By himself man, even the Christian, has not the slightest conception of the new life that comes from God; it surpasses all his thoughts. His own perverted thoughts of the way to serve and to please God—namely, by what he does and is—are so deeply rooted in him that, although he thinks that he understands and receives God's Word, he is in reality only thinking on a human level about spiritual thoughts.[5] Not only must God give salvation and life; He must also give His Spirit to help us understand what He gives. Not only must He point out the land of Canaan and the way to it; we must also be led every day by Him within the land.

The new believer must allow the Holy Spirit to show him his ignorance concerning the new life and of his inability to form right thoughts about it. This will bring him to the meekness and to the childlike spirit of teachableness by which the Lord can make His secret known.[6]

There is a second hindrance in the way of faith. In the life of every plant and every animal and every child there lies sufficient power by which it can grow. In the new life, God has made the most glorious provision of sufficient power by which His child can grow and become all that he must be. Christ himself is his life and his power of life.[7] Yet, because this mighty life is not visible or cannot be felt—but works

---

[4]John 10:10, 28; Heb. 7:16, 28; 11:25, 26; 2 Cor. 12:9; 13:4; Col. 3:3, 4; Phil. 4:13

[5]Josh. 3:4; Isa. 4:5, 6; Matt. 16:23

[6]Ps. 25:5, 8, 9; 143:8; Isa. 42:16; 64:4; Matt. 11:25; 1 Cor. 1:18, 19; 2:7, 10, 12; Heb. 11:8

[7]Ps. 18:2; 27:1; 36:8, 9; John 14:19; Gal. 2:20; Col. 3:3, 4

in the midst of human weakness—the young Christian often becomes of doubtful mind. This second hindrance, then, is that *he fails to believe that he shall grow* with divine power and certainty. He does not understand that the believing life is a life of faith whereby he depends upon the life that is in Christ for him, although he neither sees, feels, nor experiences anything.[8]

Let everyone then that has received this new life cultivate this great conviction: It is eternal life that works in me; it works with divine power; I can and shall become what God will have me be; Christ himself is my life; I receive Him every day as the life of God in me, and He shall be my life in full power.

O my Father, you have given me your Son that I may have life in Him. I thank you for the glorious new life that is now in me. Teach me to understand this new life. I acknowledge my ignorance and the perverted thoughts which are in me concerning your ways. I will believe in the heavenly power of the new life that is in me; I will believe that my Lord Jesus, who himself is my life, will by His Spirit teach me to know how I can walk in that life. Amen.

Meditate upon the following lessons in your heart:

1. It is eternal life, the very life of God, that you have now received through faith.

2. This new life in Christ, through the Holy Spirit, is in you to communicate to you all that is in Christ. Christ lives in you through the Holy Spirit.

3. This life is a life of wonderful power. However weak you may feel, believe in the divine power of the life that is in you.

4. This life needs time to grow in you and to take possession of you. Give it time; it will surely become greater.

5. Do not forget that the rules and the ways of this new

---

[8]Hab. 2:4; Matt. 6:27; Rom. 1:17; Gal. 3:11; Heb. 10:38

life are in conflict with all human thoughts of the way to please God. Be careful to guard against old ways of thinking, and let Christ, who is your life and also your wisdom, teach you all things.

CHAPTER 2

The Milk of the Word

"As newborn babes, desire the sincere milk of the word, that ye may grow thereby" (1 Pet. 2:2).

As new believers, listen carefully to what your Father has to say in this verse. You have only recently given yourselves to the Lord and have believed that He has received you. You have received the new life from God. You are now as newborn infants. He would teach you in this verse what is necessary for you to grow and become strong.

The first point is this: *You must know that you are God's children.* Hear how distinctly Peter says this to those just converted:[1] "You have been born again," "you are newborn infants," "you are now converted," "you are now the people of God." A Christian, however young and weak he may be, must *know* that he is God's child. Then only can he have the courage to believe that he will make progress and will have the boldness to use the food of the children provided in the Word. All scripture teaches us that we must know and can know that we are children of God.[2] The assurance of faith is indispensable to a healthy, powerful growth in the Lord.[3]

The second point which this word teaches you is that *you are still very weak*, weak like newborn children. The joy and the love which a new believer sometimes experiences often makes him think that he is very strong. He runs the risk of

---

[1] 1 Pet. 1:23; 2:2, 10, 25
[2] Rom. 8:16; 1 Cor. 3:1, 16; Gal. 4:6, 7; 1 John 3:2, 14, 24; 4:13; 5:10, 13
[3] Eph. 5:8; Col. 2:6; 1 Pet. 1:14, 18, 19

17

exalting himself and of trusting in what he experiences. He must nevertheless learn how to become strong in his Lord Jesus. It is important to acknowledge that you are still young and weak.[4] Out of this sense of weakness comes the humility which has nothing[5] in itself and therefore expects all from its Lord.[6]

The third lesson is this: *The new believer must not remain weak.* He must grow and increase in grace; he must make progress and become strong. This has come to us as God's command. His Word gives us concerning this point the most glorious promises. The command lies in the nature of the thing: a child of God must and can make progress. The new life is a life that is healthy and strong. When a disciple surrenders himself to it, the growth certainly comes.[7]

The fourth and principal lesson, the lesson which new believers have most need of, is this: *It is through the milk of the Word that God's newborn infants can grow.* The new life from the Spirit of God can be sustained only by the Word that God has spoken. Your spiritual life will largely depend upon whether you learn to deal wisely and handle carefully God's Word—whether you learn to use the Word from the beginning as your milk.[8]

The Lord has given us a charming parable here on the mother's milk. Out of her own life does the mother yield food and life to her child. The feeding of the child is the work of the tenderest love, in which the child is pressed to the breast and is held in the closest fellowship with the mother. And the milk is just what the weak child requires—food that is gentle and yet strong.

Even so there is in the Word of God the very life and power of God.[9] His tender love will work through the Word

---

[4]1 Cor. 3:1, 13; Heb. 5:13, 14

[5]Matt. 5:3; Rom. 12:3, 10; Eph. 4:2; Phil. 2:3, 4; Col. 3:12

[6]Matt. 8:8, 15, 27, 28

[7]Judg. 5:31; Ps. 84:7; 92:13, 14; Prov. 4:18; Isa. 40:31; Eph. 4:14; 1 Thess. 4:1; 2 Pet. 3:18

[8]Ps. 19:8, 11; 119:97, 100; Isa. 55:2, 3; 1 Cor. 12:11

[9]John 6:63; 1 Thess. 2:13; Heb. 4:12

and bring us into the gentlest and most intimate fellowship with himself.[10] His love will give us out of the Word what, like the mother's milk, is properly suited to meet our weakness. Never think that the Word is too difficult or too hard for you. For the disciple who receives the Word and trustfully relies on Jesus to teach him by the Spirit, the Word of God will practically prove to be gentle sweet milk for newborn infants.[11]

Dear new believers, would you continue standing, would you become strong, would you always live for the Lord? Then hear the voice of your Father: "As newborn babes, desire the sincere milk of the word." Receive this Word into your heart and hold it fast as the voice of your Father; your spiritual life depends upon how you use His Word, His thoughts toward you. Let the Word of God be precious to you above everything.[12]

Above all, do not forget this: The Word is the milk; the sucking or drinking on the part of the little child is the inner, living, blessed fellowship with the mother's love. Through the Holy Spirit your use of the milk of the Word can become the warm, living fellowship with the love of your God. Oh, desire then, very eagerly, for the milk. Do not view the Word as something that is hard and troublesome to understand; in that way you lose all delight in it. Receive it with trust in the love of the living God. With a tender motherly love the Spirit of God will teach and help you in your weakness. Believe always that the Spirit will make the Word in you life and joy, a blessed fellowship with your God.

Precious Savior, you have taught me to believe your word, and you have made me your child by that faith. Through that Word, as with milk to newborn babes, feed me. Lord, I am very eager to receive your Word; every day will I long after it. Teach me, through the Holy Spirit and the Word, to walk

[10]John 10:4
[11]Ps. 119:18; John 14:26; Eph. 1:17, 18
[12]Ps. 119:14, 47, 48, 111, 127

every day in living fellowship with the love of the Father. Teach me always to believe that your Spirit has been given to me with the Word. Amen.

1. Which verses did you consider the best for proving that the Scriptures teach us that we must know we are children of God?

2. What are the three points in which the sucking child is to us a type of the new believer in his dealing with the Word?

3. What must a new believer do when he senses little blessing in the reading of God's Word? (He must maintain that it is through faith that he is in fellowship with Jesus Christ; he must count on the fact that Jesus will teach him through the Spirit and so trustfully continue the reading.)

4. Remember: one verse that meets a need in your life which is read ten times and then stored in the heart is better than ten verses read once. It is only the Word that I actually receive and inwardly appropriate for myself that becomes food for my soul.

5. Select a verse that you consider one of the most glorious promises about making progress and becoming strong; memorize it and repeat it continually as the language of your positive expectation.

6. Have you fully understood what the great means for growth in grace is?

CHAPTER 3

God's Word in Our Heart

"Therefore shall ye lay up these my words in your heart and in your soul" (Deut. 11:18).

"Son of man, all my words that I shall speak unto thee receive in thine heart" (Ezek. 3:10).

"Thy word have I hid in mine heart, that I might not sin against thee" (Ps. 119:11).

Intensely desire the milk "that ye may grow thereby." This charming word must be taught to every new believer: if he would grow, he must receive the Word as milk, as the living participation of the life and the love of God. On this account it is of so great importance to understand how we must handle the Word. The Lord says that we must receive it and store it up in our heart.[1] The Word must possess and fill the heart. What does it mean?

The heart is the temple of God. In the temple there was an outer court and an inner sanctuary. So also is it in the heart. The gate of the court is the understanding; what I do not understand cannot enter into the heart. Through the outer gate of the understanding, the Word comes into the court.[2] There it is kept by memory and reflection.[3] But, it is not yet properly in the heart. From the court there is an entrance into the innermost sanctuary; the entrance of the

---

[1] Deut. 30:14; Ps. 1:2; 119:34, 36; Isa. 51:7; John 5:38; 8:31; 15:7; Rom. 10:8, 9; Col. 3:16

[2] Ps. 119:34; Matt. 13:19; Acts 8:30

[3] Ps. 119:15, 16

door is *faith*. What I believe, that I receive into my heart.[4] Here it then becomes held fast in love and in the surrender of the will. Where this takes place, there the heart becomes the sanctuary of God. His law is there, as in the ark, and the soul cries out, "Thy law is within my heart."[5]

New believer, God has asked for your heart, your love, your whole self. You have given yourself to Him. He has received you and would have you and your heart entirely for himself. He desires that your heart would become full of His Word. What is in the heart one holds dear, because one thinks continually on that which gives joy. God would have the Word in the heart. Where His Word is, there is He himself and His power. He is always faithful to fulfill His Word; when you have the Word, you have God himself to work in you.[6] He desires that you receive and treasure His words in your heart; then will He greatly bless you.[7]

How I wish that I could bring all new believers to receive simply that word of their Father, "Lay up these my words in your heart," and to give their whole heart to become full of God's Word. Determine to do this. Take pains to understand what you read. When you understand it, then take that word into your heart to keep it in remembrance. Learn words of God by heart; repeat them to yourself in the course of the day. The Word is seed. As the seed must have time, must be kept in the ground, so must the Word be carried in the heart. Give the best powers of your heart, your love, your desire, the willing and joyful activity of your will to God's Word.

"Blessed is the man whose delight is in the law of the Lord; and in his law doth he meditate day and night." Let the heart be a temple, not for the world its thoughts, but for God and His thoughts.[8] Those who faithfully open their hearts to hear God's voice, and keep and carry about that word, shall see how faithfully God also shall open His heart to their

---

[4]John 5:38; Acts 8:37; Rom. 10:10, 17
[5]Ex. 25:16; Ps. 37:31; 40:8; Col. 3:16
[6]Gen. 21:1; Josh. 23:14
[7]Deut. 11:10; 28:1, 2; Ps. 1:2, 3; 119:14, 45, 98, 165; John 17:6, 8, 17
[8]Ps. 119:69; John 15:3, 7; 17:6, 8, 17

voices, to hear what they say to Him in prayer.

Dear believer, read yet once again the verses at the beginning of this section. Receive them as God's voice to you—the word of the Father who has received you as a child, of Jesus who has made you God's child. God asks of you, as His child, that you give your heart to become filled with His Word. Will you do this?

The Lord Jesus will powerfully complete His holy work in you along this way.[9] Let your answer be distinct and continuous: "I have hid thy word in my heart"; "How love I thy law: it is my meditation all the day." When it seems difficult to understand the Word, read it over and over. The Father has promised to make it a blessing in your heart. But you must first take it into your heart. Believe then that God will by the Holy Spirit make it living and powerful in you.

O my Father, you have said, "My son, give me thine heart." I have given you my heart. Now I see that your command for me is to lay up and to keep your Word in my heart. I answer: "I keep thy commands with my whole heart." Father, teach me daily to receive your Word into my heart that it can exercise there its blessed influence. Strengthen me in the deep conviction that even though I do not fully understand its meaning and power, I can still depend upon you to make the Word living and powerful in me. Amen.

1. What is the difference between reading the Word to increase knowledge and receiving it in faith?

2. The Word is as a seed. Seed requires time to spring up. During this time it must be kept silently and constantly in the earth. I must not only read God's Word, but I must ponder and reflect upon it. Then it will work in me. The Word must be in me the whole day, must abide in me, must dwell in me.

3. What are the reasons that the Word of God sometimes has so little power in those that read it and really long for

---

[9]John 14:21, 23; 1 John 2:14, 24; Rev. 3:8, 10

blessing? (One of the principal reasons is that they do not give the seed time to grow, that they do not keep it and reflect upon it in the believing assurance that the Word itself will have its working.)

4. What is the characteristic of His disciples that Jesus mentions first in the high priestly prayer? (John 17)

5. What are the blessings of a heart filled with the Word of God?

CHAPTER 4

Faith

"Blessed is she that believed; for there shall be a perfor-
mance of those things which were told her from the Lord"
(Luke 1:45).

"I believe God, that it shall be even as it was told me" (Acts
27:25).

"[Abraham] was strong in faith, . . . being fully persuaded
that, what he had promised, he was able also to perform"
(Rom. 4:20, 21).

God has asked you to take and treasure His words in your
heart. Faith is the proper avenue whereby the Word is taken
and received into the innermost depths of the heart. Let the
new believer then take pains always to understand better
what faith is; he will thereby gain an insight into the reasons
why such great things are bound up with faith. He will yield
his perfect agreement to the view that full salvation is made
daily to be dependent on faith.[1]

Let me ask my reader to read over once again the three
verses which stand above, and to find out what is the primary
thought they teach about faith. Read nothing into them, but
simply read these words of God and ask yourself what they
teach you about faith.

They help us see that faith always attaches itself to what
God has said or promised. When an honorable man says any-
thing, he also does it; back of the saying follows the doing.
So also it is with God: when He would do anything, He says

---

[1] 2 Chron. 20:20; Mark 9:23; Heb. 11:33, 35; 1 John 5:4, 5

so first in His Word. When the believer becomes possessed with this conviction and established in it, God always does for him what He has said. With God, speaking and doing always go together; the deed follows the word. "Shall he say it, and not do it?"[2] When I have a word of God in which He promises to do something, I can always be certain that He will do it. I have simply to take and hold fast the word, and wait upon God. God will take care that He fulfills His word to me. Before I ever feel or experience anything, I hold fast the promise; and I know by faith that God will make it good to me.[3]

What is faith? None other than the certainty that what God says is true. When God says that something exists or is, then faith rejoices, although it sees nothing of it.[4] When God says that He has given me something, that something in heaven is mine—I know by faith with entire certainty that it is mine.[5] When God says that something shall come to pass, or that He will do something for me, this is for faith just as good as if I had seen it.[6] Things that are, but that I have not seen, and things that are not yet, but shall come, are for faith entirely certain. "Faith is the substance of things hoped for, the evidence [proving] of things not seen."[7] Faith always asks only for what God has said, and then relies on His faithfulness and power to fulfill His Word.

Let us now review again the words of Scripture. Of Mary we read: "Blessed is she that believed; for there shall be a performance of the things which were told her from the Lord." All things that have been spoken in the Word shall be fulfilled for me; so I believe them.

Of Abraham it is reported that he was fully assured that that which had been promised, God was also able to fulfill.

---

[2]Gen. 21:1; 32:12; Num. 14:17, 18, 20; 23:19; Josh. 21:45; 23:14; 2 Sam. 7:25, 29; Ps. 119:49

[3]Luke 1:38, 45; John 3:33; 4:50; 11:40; 20:29; Heb. 11:11, 18

[4]Rom. 1:17; 4:5; 5:1; Gal. 3:27; Eph. 1:19; 3:17

[5]John 3:16, 17, 36; 1 John 5:12, 13

[6]Rom. 8:38; Phil. 3:21; 1 Thess. 5:24; 1 Pet. 1:4, 5

[7]Heb. 11:1

This is assurance of faith—to be assured that God will do what He has promised.

This is precisely stated in the words of Paul: "I believe God, that it shall be even as it was told me." It stood fixed with him that God would do what He had spoken.

New believers in Christ, the new, the eternal life that is in you, is a life of faith. And do you not see how simple and how blessed this life of faith is? I go daily to the Word and hear what God has said that He has done and will do.[8] I take time to store in my heart the word which God says; and I hold it fast, completely certain that what God has promised, He is able to perform. And then in a childlike spirit I wait for the fulfillment of all the glorious promises of His Word. And my soul experiences this word: Blessed is she that believed; for the things spoken to her from the Lord shall be fulfilled. God promises; I believe; God fulfills: that is the secret of the new life.

O my Father, I thank you for this blessed life of faith in which we are to walk. I can do nothing, but you can do all things. All that you can do, you have spoken in your Word. And every word that I take and trustfully bring to you, you fulfill. Father, in this life of faith, so simple, so glorious, will I walk with you. Amen.

1. The Christian must read and search the Scriptures to increase his knowledge. For this purpose he daily reads one or more sections of Scripture. But he reads the Scriptures also to strengthen his faith. And for this reason he must take one or two verses and make them the subject of special reflection, thus to appropriate them trustfully for himself.

2. Do not allow yourselves to be led astray by those who speak as if faith were something great and unintelligible. Faith is none other than the certainty that God speaks truth. Take the promises of God and say to Him, "I know for certain

---

[8]Gal. 2:20; 3:2, 5; 5:5, 6; Heb. 10:35; 1 Pet. 1:3

that this promise is truth, and that you will fulfill it." He will do it.

3. Never mourn over unbelief as if it were only a weakness which you cannot help. As God's child, however weak you may be, you have the power to believe, for the Spirit of God is in you. You have only to maintain this: No one understands anything unless he has the power to believe; he must simply begin and continue saying to the Lord that he is sure that His Word is truth. He must hold fast the promise and rest upon God for the fulfillment.

CHAPTER 5

The Power of God's Word

"Faith cometh by hearing, and hearing by the word of God" (Rom. 10:17).

"Receive with meekness the engrafted word, which is able to save your souls" (James 1:21).

"We thank God without ceasing, because, when ye received the word of God which ye heard of us, ye received it not as the word of men, but as it is in truth, the word of God, which effectually worketh also in you that believe" (1 Thess. 2:13).

"For the word of God is quick and powerful" (Heb. 4:12).

The new life of a child of God depends so much on the proper use of God's Word that I shall once again speak of it to new believers.

It is a great discovery when the believer discerns that he can receive and accomplish the new life only through faith. He has only to believe; God will fulfill what is promised. Every morning he affirms his trust in Jesus and in the new life working in him; Jesus will see that the new life accomplishes what He has promised.

But now he runs the risk of another error. He thinks the faith that does such great things must be something great, and that he must have great power in order to exercise such a great faith.[1] And, because he does not feel this power, he thinks he cannot believe as he should. This error may prove to follow him his entire life.

Come and hear, then, how perverted this thought is. You

---

[1] Luke 17:5, 6; Rom. 10:6–8

need not bring this mighty faith to get the Word fulfilled, but the Word comes and strengthens the faith which you must have. "The word is living and powerful." The Word works faith in you. The Scripture says, "Faith is by the word."[2]

Think on what we have said of the heart as a temple and of its two divisions. There is the outer court, with the understanding as its gate or entrance. There is the innermost sanctuary, with the faith of the heart as its entrance. There is a natural faith—the historic faith—which every man has; with this I first receive the Word into my keeping and consideration. I must say to myself, "The Word of God is certainly true. I can stand upon it." Thus I bring the Word into the outer court, and from within the heart desire reaches out to it, seeking to receive it into the heart. The Word now exercises its divine power of life: it begins to grow and shoot out roots. As a seed which I place in the earth sends forth roots and presses still deeper into the soil, the Word presses inwardly into the holy place. The Word thus works true saving faith.[3]

New believer, understand this. The Word is living and powerful; through the Word you are born again. The Word works faith in you; through the Word faith is stimulated. Receive the Word simply with the thought that it will work in you. Keep yourselves occupied with the Word, and give it time. The Word has a divine life in itself; carry it in your inmost parts, and it will work life in you. It will work in you a faith strong and able for anything.

Beware of the lie that comes, "I cannot believe." You *can* believe. You have the Spirit of God in you. Even the natural man can say, "This Word of God is certainly true." And when he with a desire of the soul says, "It is true; I will believe it," the living Spirit, through whom the Word is living and powerful, works this living faith. Besides, the Spirit is not only in the Word but also in you. Although you do not feel as if

---

[2]Rom. 10:17; Heb. 4:12
[3]1 Thess. 2:13; James 1:21; 1 Pet. 1:23

you were believing, know for certain you can believe.[4] Begin actually to receive the Word; it will work a mighty faith in you. Rely upon the fact that with God's Word, you have a word that can be surely trusted to work powerfully with your faith.

And not only the promises, but also the commands have this living power. When I first receive a command from God, it is as if I feel no power to accomplish it. But if I simply receive it as God's Word, which works in those who believe— if I trust in the Word to have its working and in the living God who gives it its operation—that commandment will work in me the desire and the power for obedience. When I hold fast the command, it works the desire and the will to obey; it urges me strongly toward the conviction that I can certainly do what my Father says. The Word works to energize both faith and obedience. The obedience of the Christian is the obedience of faith. I must believe that through the Spirit I have the power to do what God wills, for in the Word the power of God works in me. The Word, as the command of the living God who loves me, is my power.[5]

Therefore, new believer, learn to receive God's Word trustfully. Although you do not at first understand it, continue to meditate upon it. It has a living power in it; it will glorify itself. Although you feel no power to believe or to obey, the Word is living and powerful. Take it and hold it fast. It will accomplish its work with divine power. The Word rouses and strengthens for faith and obedience.

Lord God, I have begun to understand that you are in your Word with life and power, and that your Word itself strengthens faith and obedience in the heart that receives and keeps it. Lord, teach me to carry your every word as a living seed in my heart in the assurance that it will work in me all your good pleasure.

---

[4]Deut. 32:46, 47; Josh. 1:7, 9
[5]Gal. 6:6; 1 Thess. 1:3; James 1:21

1. Remember: it is one and the same to believe in the Word, or in the person that speaks the Word, or in the thing which is promised in the Word. The very same faith that receives the promises receives also the Father who promises and the Son with the salvation which is given in the promises. You never separate the Word and the living God from each other.

2. Remember: there is a great distinction between the reception of the Word "as the word of man" and "as the word of God, which works in you that believe."

3. I think that you now know what is necessary to become strong in faith. Exercise as much faith as you have. Take a promise of God. Say to yourself that it is certainly true. Go to God and say to Him that you rely on Him for the fulfillment. Ponder the promise and cleave to it in fellowship with God. Rely on Him to do for you what He says. He will surely do it.

4. Remember: the Spirit and the Word always go together. All that the Word says I *must* do, I can be sure that I *can* do it through the Spirit. I must receive the Word and also the command in the confidence that it is the Word of the living God which also works in us who believe.

CHAPTER 6

God's Gift of His Son

"For God so loved the world, that he gave his only begotten Son, that whosoever believeth in him should not perish, but have everlasting life" (John 3:16).

"Thanks be unto God for his unspeakable gift" (2 Cor. 9:15).

Thus dearly did God hold the world. How dearly? That He gave His only begotten Son for everyone in the world. And how did He give? He gave Him in His birth as man in order to be forever one with us. He gave Him in His death on the cross in order to take our sin and curse upon himself. He gave Him on the throne of heaven in order to arrange for our welfare as our representative and intercessor over all the powers of heaven. He gave Him in the outpouring of the Spirit in order to dwell in us, to be entirely and altogether our own.[1] Yes, that is the love of God—that He gave His Son to us, for us, in us.

Nothing less than His Son himself—that is the love of God; not that He gives us something but that He gives us someone—a living person; not one or another blessing but Him in whom is all life and blessing—Jesus himself; not simply forgiveness, or revival, or sanctification, or glory, but Jesus, His own Son.

The Lord Jesus is the beloved, the equal, the bosom-friend, the eternal blessedness of the Father. And it is the will of

---

[1]John 1:14, 16; 14:23; Rom. 5:8; 8:32, 34; Eph. 1:22; 3:17; Col. 2:9, 10; Heb. 7:24, 26; 1 John 4:9, 10

the Father that we should have Jesus as ours, even as He has Him.[2] For this purpose God gave Him to us. The whole of salvation consists in this: to have, to possess, to enjoy Jesus. God has given His Son—given Him wholly to become ours.[3]

What have we, then, to do? To take Him, to receive and to appropriate to ourselves the gift, to enjoy Jesus as our own. This is eternal life. "He that hath the Son hath life."[4]

How I do wish, then, that all new believers might understand this. The one great work of God's love for us is that He gives us His Son. In Him we have all. Hence the one great work of our heart must be to receive this Jesus who has been given to us, to consider Him and appropriate Him as ours.

I must begin every day with the thought: I have Jesus to do all for me.[5] In all weakness or darkness or danger, in the case of every desire or need, let your first thought always be: I have Jesus to make everything right for me, for God has given Him to me. Whether you need forgiveness or consolation or confirmation; whether you have fallen, or are tempted to fall into danger; whether you do not understand what the will of God is in one or another matter, or know that you have not the courage and the strength to do this will—let this always be your first thought: the Father has given me Jesus to care for me.

For this purpose, depend upon this gift of God every day as yours. It has been presented to you in the Word. Appropriate the Son in faith on the Word. Affirm your faith in Him every day—through faith you have the Son.[6] The love of God has given the Son. Take Him and hold Him fast in the love of your heart.[7] It is to bring life, eternal life, to you that God has given Jesus. Take Him up into your life; let your heart

---

[2]Matt. 11:27; John 17:23, 25; Rom. 8:38, 39; Heb. 2:11
[3]Ps. 73:24; 142:6; John 20:28; Heb. 3:14
[4]John 1:12; 2 Cor. 3:5; Col. 2:6; 1 John 5:12
[5]John 15:5; Rom. 8:37; 1 Cor. 1:30; Eph. 1:3; 2:10; Phil. 4:13; 2 Tim. 1:12
[6]John 1:12; 1 John 5:9, 13
[7]1 John 4:4, 19

and your tongue and your whole life be under the power and guidance of Jesus.[8]

New believer, listen to that Word. God has given you Jesus. He is yours. Receiving is nothing but the fruit of faith. The gift is for you. He will do all for you.

O my Lord Jesus, today anew, and every day, I receive you. In all your fullness, in all your relations, without ceasing, I take you for myself. You are my wisdom, my light, my leader— I take you as my prophet. You have perfectly reconciled me and brought me near to God. You purify and sanctify me and pray for me—I take you as my priest. You guide and keep and bless me—I take you as my king. You are my all in all, and you are wholly mine. Thanks be to God for His unspeakable gift. Amen.

1. Meditate on the word "give." God gives in a wonderful way—from the heart, completely for nothing, to the unworthy. And He gives effectually. What He gives He will really make entirely our possession and inwardly appropriate for us. Believe this, and you shall have the certainty that Jesus will completely come into your possession with all that He brings.

2. Meditate also on that other word "take." To take Jesus, and to hold Him fast and to appropriate Him, is our great work. And that receiving is nothing but trusting. He is mine with all that He has. Take Jesus—the full Jesus—every day as yours. This is the secret of the life of faith.

3. Then consider also the word "have." "He that hath the Son hath life." What I have is mine, for my use and service. I can have the full enjoyment of it. "He that hath the Son hath life."

4. Mark especially that what God gives, and what you take, and what you now have is nothing less than the living Son of God.

Do you receive this?

---

[8]2 Cor. 5:15; Phil. 3:8

CHAPTER 7

Jesus' Surrender of Himself

"Christ also loved the church, and gave himself for it; that he might sanctify ... that he might present it to himself a glorious church, not having spot, or wrinkle, or any such thing; but that it should be holy and without blemish" (Eph. 5:25–27).

So great and wonderful was the work that Jesus had to do for the sinner that it was necessary that He should give himself to do that work. So great and wonderful was the love of Jesus toward us that He actually gave himself for us and to us. So great and wonderful is the surrender of Jesus that all He gave himself to accomplish for us can actually and completely come to pass in us. For Jesus, the holy, the almighty, has taken it upon himself to do it: He gave *himself* for us.[1] And now the one thing that is necessary is that we understand and firmly believe His surrender for us.

To what end, then, was it that He gave himself for the Church? Hear what God says: it was in order that He might sanctify it; in order that it might be without blemish.[2] This is the aim of Jesus. This purpose He will accomplish in the believer who makes this his highest desire, and then relies upon Jesus' surrender of himself to do it.

Hear still a word of God: "Who gave himself for us, that he might redeem us from all iniquity, and purify unto him-

---

[1]Gal. 1:4; 2:20; Eph. 5:2, 25; 1 Tim. 2:6; Titus 2:14
[2]Eph. 1:4; 5:27; Col. 1:22; 1 Thess. 2:10; 3:13; 5:23, 24

self a peculiar people, zealous of good works."[3] Yes, it is to prepare for himself a *pure* people, a people *of His own*, a *zealous* people, that Jesus gives himself. When I receive Him, when I believe that He gave himself to do this for me, I shall certainly experience it. I shall be purified through Him, shall be held fast as His possession, and be filled with zeal and joy to work for Him.

And notice, further, how the goal of this surrender of himself is that He shall then have us entirely for himself: That He might present us to himself, that He might purify us to himself, a people of His own. The more I understand and contemplate Jesus' surrender of himself for me, the more I give myself again to Him. The surrender is a mutual one; the love comes from both sides. His giving of himself makes such an impression on my heart that my heart with the self-same love and joy becomes entirely His. Through giving himself to me, He of himself takes possession of me; He becomes mine and I His. I know that I have Jesus wholly for me, and that He has me wholly for Him.[4]

How, then, shall I come to the full enjoyment of this blessed life? "I live in faith, *the faith* which is in the Son of God, who loved me and gave himself up for me."[5] Through faith I reflect upon and contemplate His surrender for me as certain and glorious. Through faith I appropriate it. Through faith I trust in Jesus to confirm this surrender, to communicate himself to me and reveal himself within me. Through faith I wait with certainty for the full experience of salvation which arises from having Jesus as mine, to do all for me. Through faith I live in this Jesus who loved me and gave himself for me. And I say, "No longer do I live, but Christ liveth in me." Christian, believe it with your whole heart: Jesus gives himself for you; He is wholly yours; He will do all for you.[6]

---

[3]Titus 2:14
[4]Ex. 19:4, 5; Deut. 26:17, 18; Isa. 41:9, 10; 1 Cor. 6:19, 20; 1 Pet. 2:10
[5]John 6:29, 35; 7:38; 10:10, 38; Gal. 2:20
[6]Matt. 8:10; 9:2, 22; Mark 11:24; Luke 7:50; 8:48; 17:19; 18:42; Rom. 4:20, 21; 5:2; 11:20; Gal. 3:25, 26; Eph. 1:19; 3:17

O my Lord Jesus, what wonderful grace is this, that you gave yourself for me. You are eternal life. You are the life and you give yourself to be in my life all that I need. You purify me and sanctify me and make me zealous in good works. You take me wholly for yourself, and give yourself wholly for me. Yes, my Lord, in all you are my life. Oh, help me to understand this. Amen.

1. It was in His great love that the Father gave the Son. It was out of love that Jesus gave himself (Rom. 3:16; Eph. 5:26). The taking, the having of Jesus, is the entrance to a life in the love of God; this is the highest life (John 14:21, 23; 17:23, 26; Eph. 3:17, 18). Through faith we must press into love, and dwell there (1 John 4:16–18).

2. Have you learned the lesson, to begin every day with the childlike trust: I take Jesus this day to be my life and to do all for me?

3. Understand that to take and to have Jesus presupposes a personal dealing with him. To have pleasure in Him, to have fellowship with Him, to rejoice in Him as my friend and in His love—to this leads the faith that truly takes Him.

CHAPTER 8

Children of God

"As many as received him, to them gave he power to become the sons of God, even to them that believe on his name" (John 1:12).

What is given must be received; otherwise it is of no benefit. If the first great deed of God's love is the gift of His Son, the first work of man must be to receive this Son. And if all the blessings of God's love come to us only in the ever-living Son of the Father, all these blessings enter into us from day to day through the always-new, always-continuing reception of the Son.

You know what is necessary for this reception, for you have already received the Lord Jesus. But all that this reception involves must become clearer and stronger, the unceasing living action of your faith.[1] Our faith must increase if we are to grow. Your first receiving of Jesus rested on the certainty which the Word gave you—that He was for you. Through the Word your life must be still further filled with the assurance that all that is in Christ is literally and really for you, given by the Father in Him to be your life.

Your first receiving of Christ was prompted by your want and necessity. Through the Spirit you become still poorer in spirit, and you see more intensely how you need Jesus for everything every moment; this leads to a ceaseless, ever-active taking of Him as your all.[2]

---

[1] 2 Cor. 10:15; 1 Thess. 1:8, 3:10; 2 Thess. 1:3
[2] Matt. 5:3; 1 Cor. 3:10, 13, 16; Eph. 4:14, 15; Col. 2:6

Your first receiving consisted in nothing but the appropriation by faith of what you could not yet see or feel. The same faith must be continually exercised in saying: "All that I see in Jesus is for me. I take it as mine although I do not yet experience it." The love of God is a communicating, a ceaseless outstreaming of His light of life over the soul, a very powerful and true giving of Jesus. Our life is nothing but a continuous blessed apprehension and reception of Him.[3]

And this is the way to live as children of God; as many as receive Him, to them He gives the power to become children of God. This holds true not only of conversion and regeneration but of every day of my life. If to walk in all things as a child of God and to exhibit the image of my Father is indispensable, I must take Jesus, the only begotten Son; it is He that makes me a child of God. To have Jesus himself, to have the heart and life full of Him, is the way to live as a child of God. I go to the Word and learn there all the characteristics of a child of God.[4] And after each of them I write: This Jesus shall work in me; I *have* Him to make me to be a child of God.

Beloved new believer, learn to understand the simplicity and the glory of being a true Christian. It is to receive Jesus, to receive Him in all His fullness, to receive Him in all the glorious relations in which the Father gives Him to you. Take Him as your prophet, as your wisdom, your light, your guide. Take Him as your priest, who renews you, purifies you, sanctifies you, brings you near to God, takes you and forms you wholly for His service. Take Him as your king who governs you, protects you and blesses you. Take Him as your head, your example, your brother, your life, your all.

The giving of God is a divine, ever-progressive and effectual communication to your soul. Let your receiving be the childlike, cheerful, continuous opening of mouth and heart for what God gives—the full Jesus and all His grace. To every

---

[3]John 1:16; Col. 2:9, 10; 3:3

[4]Matt. 5:9, 16, 44, 45; Rom. 8:14; Eph. 1:4, 5; 5:1, 2; Phil. 2:15; Heb. 2:10; 1 Pet. 1:14, 17; 1 John 3:1, 10; 5:1, 3

prayer the answer of God is Jesus, all is in Him; all in Him is for you. Let your response always be Jesus, in Him I have all. You are, you live in all things as "children of God, through faith in Jesus Christ."

O my Father, open the eyes of my heart to understand what it is to be a child of God, to live always as a child through always believing in Jesus, your only Son. Oh, let every breath of my soul be faith in Jesus, a confidence in Him, a resting in Him, a surrender to Him, to work all in me.

1. Remember: all that the Father has provided for us is found in Jesus. We are to be in the always-new, always-continuing reception of the Son.

2. What is the only way to live as children of God?

CHAPTER 9

Our Surrender to Jesus

"They . . . gave their own selves to the Lord" (2 Cor. 8:5).

In the surrender of Jesus for me, I have the chief element of what He has done and always does for me. In my surrender to Him, I have the chief element of what He would have me to do. For new believers who have given themselves to Jesus, it is of great importance always to hold fast, to confirm and renew this surrender. This is the life of faith, to say anew every day, "I have given myself to Him, to follow Him and to serve Him.[1] He has taken me. I am His and entirely at His service."[2]

New believer, hold firm your surrender, and strengthen it. When there occurs a stumbling or a sin after you have surrendered yourself, do not think the surrender was not sincere. No, the surrender to Jesus does not make us perfect at once. You have sinned because you were not thoroughly or firmly enough in His arms. Reaffirm this, although it be with shame: "Lord, you know that I have given myself to you; I am yours."[3] Confirm this surrender again. Tell Him that you now see clearer how complete the surrender to Him must be, and renew every day the voluntary, entire, and undivided offering up of yourselves to Him.[4]

As we grow as believers, the deeper will be our insight

---

[1]Matt. 4:22; 10:24, 25, 37, 38; Luke 18:22; John 12:25, 26; 2 Cor. 5:15
[2]Matt. 28:20
[3]John 21:17; Gal. 6:1; 1 Thess. 5:24; 2 Tim. 2:13; 1 John 5:16
[4]Luke 18:28; Phil. 3:7, 8

into the word "surrender to Jesus." We see more clearly that we do not yet fully understand or contemplate it. The surrender must become, especially, more undivided and trustful. The language which Ahab once used must be ours: "According to thy saying, I am thine, and all that I have" (1 Kings 20:4).

This is the language of undivided dedication: "I am thine, and all that I have." Keep nothing back. Do not hide a single sin, but confess it and forsake it. There can be no surrender without repentance.[5] Keep back no single power. Let your head with all its thinking, your mouth with all its speaking, your heart with all its feeling, your hand with all its working—let your time, your name, your influence, your property—let all be laid upon the altar.[6] Jesus has a right to all; He demands the whole. Give yourself, with all that you have, to be guided and used and kept, sanctified and blessed. "According to thy saying, I am thine, and all that I have."

That is the language of trustful dedication. It is on the Word of the Lord, which calls upon you to surrender yourself, that you have done this. That Word is your guarantee that He will take and guide and keep you. As surely as you give yourself, does He take you; and what He takes He can keep. But we must not take it again out of His hand. Let it remain permanent. Remember that your surrender is in the highest degree pleasing to Him; be certain that your offering is a sweet-smelling savour. Not on what you are, or what you experience or discover in yourselves, do you say this, but on His Word.

According to His Word, you are able to stand on this: what you give, that He takes; and what He takes, that He keeps.[7] Therefore let this daily be the childlike joyful activity of your life of faith: you surrender yourselves without ceasing to Jc sus, and you are safe in the certainty that He in His love takes and holds you fast, and that His answer to your giving

---

[5]Matt. 7:21, 27; John 3:20, 21; 2 Tim. 2:19, 21

[6]Rom. 6:13, 22; 12:1; 2 Cor. 5:15; Heb. 13:15; 1 Pet. 2:5

[7]John 10:28; 2 Thess. 3:3; 2 Tim. 1:12

44

is the renewed and always deeper surrender of himself to you.

According to your Word, my Lord and King, I am yours, and all that I have. Every day, this day, will I confirm it— that I am not my own but am my Lord's. Fervently do I ask you to take full possession of your property, so that no one may doubt whose I am. Amen.

1. Ponder once again the words "giving" and "taking" and "having." What I give to Jesus He takes with a divine taking. And what He takes He thereafter cares for. Now it is absolutely no longer mine. I must not take thought for it; I may not dispose of it. Oh, let your faith find expression in adoration—Jesus takes me! Jesus has me!

2. Should there come upon you a time of doubting or darkness whereby your assurance that the Lord has received you seems to be lost, do not allow yourself thereby to be discouraged. If there is sin in your life, confess your sin; believe in His promises that He will by no means cast out those that come to Him. Then simply on the ground of the promises, begin to say, "I know He has received me."

3. Do not forget what the chief element in surrender is: It is a surrender to Jesus and to His love. *Fix your eyes not upon your activity in surrender but upon Jesus*, who calls you, who takes you, who can do all for you. This is what makes faith strong.

4. Faith is always a surrender. Faith is the eye for seeing the invisible. When I look at something, I surrender myself to the impression which it makes upon me. Faith is the ear that hearkens to the voice of God. When I believe a message, I surrender myself to the influence, cheering or saddening, which it exercises upon me. When I believe in Jesus, I surrender myself to Him—in reflection, in desire, in expectation—in order that He may be in me and do that for which He has been given to me by God.

CHAPTER 10

A Savior from Sin

"Thou shalt call his name Jesus; for he shall save his people from their sins" (Matt. 1:21).

"Ye know that he was manifested to take away our sins; and in him is no sin. Whosoever abideth in him sinneth not" (1 John 3:5, 6).

It is sin that is the cause of our misery. It is sin that provoked God and brought His curse upon man. He hates sin with a perfect hatred, and will do everything to root it out.[1] It is to take away sin that God gave His Son, that Jesus gave himself.[2] It is God who sets us free, not only from punishment and curse, from disquietude and terror, but from sin itself.[3] You know that He was manifested that He might take away our sins. Let us receive the thought deep into our hearts: it is God who takes away our sins from us. The clearer we understand this, the more blessed our life will be.

All do not receive this. They seek mainly to be freed from the consequences of sin, from fear and darkness, and the punishment that sin brings.[4] But they do not come to the true rest of salvation. They do not understand that to be saved is to be freed from sin. Let us hold it fast. Jesus saves through taking away sin. Then we shall learn two things.

The first is to come to Jesus with every sin.[5] The sin that

---

[1]Deut. 27:26; Isa. 59:1, 2; Jer. 44:4; Rom. 1:18

[2]Gal. 2:4; Eph. 5:25, 27; 1 Pet. 2:24; 1 John 3:3, 8

[3]Jer. 27:9; 1 Pet. 1:2, 15, 16; 2:14; 1 John 3:8

[4]Gen. 27:34; Isa. 58:5, 6; John 6:26; James 4:3

[5]Ps. 32:5; Luke 7:38; 19:7, 8, 10; John 8:11

still attacks and overpowers you, after you have given yourself over to the Lord, must not make you lose heart. There must also be no endeavor merely in your own strength to take away and overcome sin. Bring every sin to Jesus. He has been ordained by God to take away sin. He has already brought it to nought upon the cross and broken its power.[6] It is His work, it is His desire to set you free from it. Learn always to come to Jesus with every sin. Sin is your deadly foe; if you confess it to Jesus and surrender it to Him, you shall certainly overcome it.[7]

Learn to believe the above fact firmly. The second point is this: Understand that Jesus himself is the Savior from sin. It is not you who must overcome sin with the help of Jesus, but Jesus himself—Jesus in you.[8] If you would become free from sin, if you would enjoy full salvation, let it be the one endeavor of your life to stand always in full fellowship with Jesus. Do not wait until you enter into temptation. Let your life beforehand be always through Jesus. Let His nearness be your one desire. Jesus saves from sin; to have Jesus is salvation from sin.[9]

Oh, that we could rightly understand this! Jesus will not merely save from sin as a work that He will from time to time do in us, but He will give it as a blessing through himself to us and in us.[10]

When Jesus fills me, when Jesus is all for me, sin has no hold on me: "He that abideth in him sinneth not."

Yes, sin is driven out and kept out only through the presence of Jesus. It is Jesus, Jesus himself, who through His giving himself to me and His living in me is salvation from sin.

Precious Lord, let your light stream over me, and let it become still clearer to my soul that you, you alone, are my

---

[6]Heb. 9:26

[7]Rom. 7:4, 9; 8:2; 2 Cor. 12:9; 2 Thess. 2:3

[8]Deut. 8:17, 18; Ps. 44:4, 8; John 16:33; 1 John 5:4, 5

[9]1 Cor. 15:10; Gal. 2:20; Phil. 4:13; Col. 3:3–5

[10]Ex. 29:43; John 15:4, 5; Rom. 8:10; Eph. 3:17, 18

salvation. To have you with me, in me—this keeps sin out. Teach me to bring every sin to you; let every sin drive me into a closer alliance with you. Then shall your Jesus-name become truly my salvation from sin. Amen.

1. See of what importance it is that the Christian should always grow in the revelation of personal sin.

2. For the recognition of sin there are three requirements:

   a. The constant prayer, "Examine me; make known to me my transgression and my sin" (Job 13:23; Ps. 139:23, 24).

   b. A tender conscience that is willing to be convinced of sin through the Spirit, as He also uses the conscience for this end.

   c. A very humble surrender to the Word, to think concerning sin only as God thinks.

3. The deeper knowledge of sin will be found in these results:

   a. We will call certain things sin which we previously did not regard in this light.

   b. We shall perceive more the exceedingly sinful, the detestable charactaer of sin (Rom. 7:13).

   c. With the overcoming of external sins, we will become convinced of the enemity of our own flesh against God. We see we cannot overcome it by ourselves. Then we give up all hope of being or of doing anything good, and we are turned wholly to live in faith through the Spirit.

4. Oh, let us thank God very heartily that Jesus is a Savior from sin. The power that sin has had over us Jesus now has. The place that sin has taken in the heart, Jesus will now take. "The law of the Spirit of life in Christ Jesus hath made me free from the law of sin and death."

CHAPTER 11

The Confession of Sin

"If we confess our sins, he is faithful and just to forgive us our sins, and to cleanse us from all unrighteousness" (1 John 1:9).

The one thing that God hates, that grieves Him, that He is provoked by, and that He will destroy is sin. The one thing that makes man unhappy is sin.[1] The one thing for which Jesus had to give His blood was sin. In all the communication between the sinner and God, this is the first thing that the sinner must bring to God—his sin.[2]

When you first came to Jesus, you perceived this in some measure. But you should learn to understand this lesson more deeply. The one counsel concerning sin is to bring it immediately to the only One who can take it away—God himself. You should learn that one of the greatest privileges of a child of God is the confession of sin. It is only the holiness of God that can consume sin; through confession I hand over my sin to God, lay it down on God, renounce it before God, cast it into the fiery oven of God's holy love which burns against sin like a fire. God, yes, God himself and He alone takes away sin.[3]

Many believers fail to understand this. There is a general tendency to try to cover sin, or to make it less, or to root it out only when they plan to draw near to God. They try to

---

[1] Gen. 6:5, 6; Isa. 43:24; Ezek. 33:6; Rev. 6:16, 17
[2] Judg. 10:10, 15, 16; Ezra 9:6; Neh. 9:2, 33; Jer. 3:21, 25; Dan. 9:4, 5, 20
[3] Lev. 6:21; Num. 5:7; 2 Sam. 12:13; Ps. 32:5; 38:18; 51:5, 19

cover sin with excessive repentance and self-blame, with scorn of the temptation that came to them, or otherwise with what they have done or still hope to do.[4]

New believer, if you would enjoy the gladness of complete forgiveness and a divine cleansing from sin, make sure you use correctly the confession of sin. In the true confession of sin, you have one of the most blessed privileges of a child of God, one of the deepest foundations for a powerful spiritual life.

Therefore, let your confession be a definite one.[5] The continued vague confession of sin does more harm than good. It is much better to say to God that you have nothing to confess than to try to confess what you do not know. Begin with one sin. Let it come to a complete harmony between God and you concerning this one sin. Let it be fixed with you that this sin, through confession, is placed in God's hands. You will experience that in true confession there is both power and blessing.

Let the confession be a truthful one.[6] By it deliver up the sinful deed to be laid aside. By it deliver up the sinful feeling with a view to trusting in God. Confession implies renunciation, the putting off of sin. Give up your sin that God may forgive you and cleanse you from it. Do not confess sin if you are not prepared, if you do not heartily desire to be freed from it. Confession has value *only* as it is a giving up of sin to God.

Let confession be trustful.[7] Put your confidence in God actually forgiving you and also cleansing you from sin. Continue in confession, in casting the sin of which you desire to be free into the fire of God's holiness until your soul has the firm confidence that God takes it on His own account to forgive and to cleanse away. It is this faith that really over-

---

[4]Gen. 3:12; Ex. 32:22, 24; Isa. 1:11, 5; Luke 13:26

[5]Num. 12:11; 21:7; 2 Sam. 24:10, 17; Isa. 59:12, 13; Luke 23:41; Acts 19:18, 19; 22:19, 20; 1 Tim. 1:13, 15

[6]Prov. 28:13; Lev. 26:40, 41; Jer. 31:18, 19

[7]2 Sam. 12:13; Ps. 32:5; Isa. 55:7

comes the world and sin—the faith that God in Jesus really emancipates from sin.[8]

New believer, do you understand it now? What must you do with sin, with every sin? Bring it in confession to God; give it to God. God alone takes away sin.

Lord God, what thanks shall I express for this unspeakable blessing, that I may come to you with sin. It is known to you, Lord, how sin before your holiness causes terror and flight. It is known to you how it is our first thought to have sin covered and then to come to you with our desire and endeavor for good. Lord, teach me to come to you with sin, every sin, and in confession to lay it down before you and give it up to you. Amen.

1. What is the distinction between the covering of sin by God and by man? How does man do it? How does God do it?

2. What are the great hindrances in the way of the confession of sin?
   a. Ignorance about sin.
   b. Fear to come with sin to the holy God.
   c. The endeavor to come to God with something good.
   d. Unbelief in the power of the blood and in the riches of grace.

3. Must I immediately confess a bad attitude or a lie or a wrong word, or wait until my feeling has subsided and I feel more under control? Oh, beloved, confess it immediately; come in full sinfulness to God without first desiring to make it less!

4. Is it also necessary or good to confess before man? It is indispensable if our sin has been against man. And, besides, it is often good; it is often easier to acknowledge before God than before man that I have done something (James 5:16).

---

[8]1 John 5:5

CHAPTER 12

The Forgiveness of Sins

"Blessed is he whose transgression is forgiven, whose sin is covered" (Ps. 32:1).

"Bless the Lord, O my soul ... who forgiveth all thine iniquities" (Ps. 103:2, 3).

In connection with surrender to the Lord, it was said that the first great blessing of the grace of God was this: the free, complete, everlasting forgiveness of all our sins. For the new believer it is of great importance that he should stand fast in this forgiveness of his sins and always carry the certainty of it with him. To this end he must especially consider the following truths.

The forgiveness of our sin is a complete forgiveness.[1] God does not forgive by halves. Even with man, we consider a half forgiveness no true forgiveness. The love of God is so great and the atonement in the blood of Jesus is so complete and powerful that God always forgives completely. Take time with God's Word to come under the full impression that your guilt has been completely removed. God thinks absolutely no more of your sins. "I will forgive their iniquity, and their sin will I remember no more."[2]

The forgiveness of our sin restores us entirely again to the love of God.[3] Not only does God not impute sin anymore—that is but one-half—but He imparts to us the righteousness

---

[1]Ps. 103:12; Isa. 38:17; 55:7; Mic. 7:18, 19; Heb. 10:16–18
[2]Jer. 31:34; Heb. 8:12; 10:7
[3]Hos. 14:5; Luke 15:22; Acts 26:18; Rom. 5:1, 5

of Jesus also, so that for His sake we are as dear to God as He is. Not only is wrath turned away from us, but the fullness of love now rests upon us. "I will love them freely, for mine anger is turned away from him." Forgiveness is access to all the love of God. On this account, forgiveness is also introduced to all the other blessings of redemption.

Live in the full assurance of forgiveness, and let the Holy Spirit fill your heart with the certainty and the blessedness of it, and you will have great confidence in expecting all the blessings from God. Learn from the Word of God, through the Spirit, to know God and to trust Him as the ever-forgiving God. That is His name and His glory.

To one to whom much, yea, all, is forgiven, He will also give much. He will give all.[4] Let it therefore be every day your joyful thanksgiving. "Bless the Lord, O my soul . . . who forgiveth all [mine] iniquities." Then forgiveness becomes the power of a new life: "He who is forgiven much, loves much." The forgiveness of sins, received anew in living faith every day, is a bond that binds anew to Jesus and His service.[5]

The forgiveness of former sins always gives courage to go immediately with every new sin and trustfully to receive forgiveness.[6] Look, however, to one thing: the certainty of forgiveness must not be a matter of memory or understanding but the fruit of life—living fellowship with the forgiving Father, with Jesus in whom we have forgiveness.[7] It is not enough to know that I once received forgiveness; my life must remain in the love of God, my living fellowship with Jesus by faith—this makes the forgiveness of sin always new and powerful, the joy and the life of my soul.

Lord God, this is the wonder of your grace, that you are a forgiving God. Teach me every day to know in this anew the

---

[4]Ps. 103:3; Isa. 12:1, 3; Rom. 5:10; 8:32; Eph. 1:7; 3:5

[5]John 13:14, 15; Rom. 12:1; 1 Cor. 6:20; Eph. 5:25, 26; Titus 2:14; 1 Pet. 1:17, 18

[6]Ex. 34:6, 7; Matt. 18:21; Luke 1:77, 78

[7]Eph. 2:13, 18; Phil. 3:9; Col. 1:21, 22

glory of your love. Let the Holy Spirit seal forgiveness to me as a blessing, everlasting, ever-fresh, living, and powerful. And let my life be as a song of thanksgiving. "Bless the Lord, O my soul . . . who forgiveth all thine iniquities." Amen.

1. Basically, forgiveness is one with justification. Forgiveness is the word that looks more to the relation of God as Father. Justification looks more to His acquittal as Judge. Forgiveness is a word that is more easily understood by the new believer. But he must also endeavor to understand the word justification and what the Scripture teaches about it.

2. Concerning justification we must understand:

a. That man in himself is wholly unrighteous.

b. That he cannot be justified by works—that is, pronounced righteous before the judgment seat of God.

c. That Jesus has brought in a righteousness in our place. His obedience is our righteousness.

d. That we through faith receive Him, are united with Him, and then are pronounced righteous before God.

e. That we through faith have the certainty of this, and, as justified, draw near before God.

f. That union with Jesus is a life by which we are not only pronounced righteous but are really righteous and act righteously.

3. Let the certainty of your part in justification, in the full forgiveness of your sins, and in full restoration to the love of God, be your daily confidence in drawing near to God.

CHAPTER 13

The Cleansing of Sin

"If we walk in the light, as he is in the light, we have fellowship one with another, and the blood of Jesus Christ his Son cleanseth us from all sin. If we confess our sins, he is faithful and just to forgive us our sins, and to cleanse us from all unrighteousness" (1 John 1:7, 9).

The same God who forgives sin also cleanses from it. Cleansing is a promise of God with that of forgiveness and is therefore a matter of faith. As it is indispensable, as it is impossible for man, so is cleansing as well as forgiveness certain to be obtained from God.

And what now is this cleansing? The word comes from the Old Testament. While forgiveness was a sentence of acquittal passed on the sinner, cleansing was something that happened to him and in him. Forgiveness came to him through the Word; in the case of cleansing, something was done *to* him that he could experience.[1]

Cleansing is the inner revelation of the power of God whereby we are liberated from unrighteousness, from the pollution and the working of sin. Through cleansing we obtain the blessing of a pure heart, a heart in which the Spirit can complete His operations with a view to sanctifying us and revealing God within us.[2]

Cleansing is through the blood. Forgiveness and cleans-

---

[1]Lev. 13:13; 14:7, 8; Num. 19:12; 31:23, 24; 2 Sam. 22:21, 25; Neh. 13:30; Mal. 3:3

[2]Ps. 51:12; 73:1; Matt. 5:8; 1 Tim. 1:5; 2 Tim. 2:22; 1 Pet. 1:22

ing are both through the blood. The blood in heaven breaks the condemning power of sin. The blood thereby also breaks the power of sin in the heart to hold us captive. The blood has a ceaseless operation in heaven from moment to moment. The blood has likewise a ceaseless operation in our heart to purify, to keep pure the heart into which sin seeks to penetrate through the flesh. The blood cleanses the conscience from dead works to serve the living God. The marvelous power that the blood has in heaven it has also in the heart.[3]

Cleansing is also through the Word, for the Word testifies of the blood and of the power of God.[4] Hence also cleansing is through faith. It is a divine and effectual cleansing, but it must also be received in faith if it will be experienced and felt. I believe that I am cleansed with a divine cleansing even while I confess it to God; through faith in this blessing, cleansing itself shall be my daily experience.

Cleansing is ascribed sometimes to God or the Lord Jesus; sometimes to man.[5] That is because God cleanses us by making us active in our own cleansing. Through the blood the lust that leads to sin is mortified, the certainty of power against it is awakened, and the desire and the will are thus made alive. Happy is he that understands this. He is protected against useless endeavors of self-purification in his own strength, for he knows God alone can do it. He is protected against discouragement, for he knows God will certainly do it.

What we have to lay the chief stress upon is found in two things: the desire and the reception of cleansing. The desire must be strong for a real purification. Forgiveness must be only the gateway or beginning of a holy life. I have several times remarked that the secret of progress in the service of God is a strong yearning to become free from every sin, a hunger and thirst after righteousness.[6] Blessed are such who

---

[3]John 13:10, 11; Heb. 9:14; 10:22; 1 John 1:7

[4]John 15:3

[5]Ps. 51:3; Ezek. 30:25; John 13:2; 2 Cor. 7:1; 1 Tim. 5:22; 2 Tim. 2:21; James 4:8; 1 John 3:8

[6]Ps. 19:13; Matt. 5:6

desire purity. They shall understand and receive the promise of a cleansing from God.

They learn also the place of faith in this. Through faith they know that an unseen, spiritual, heavenly, but very real, cleansing through the blood is accomplished in them by God himself.

New believer, you remember how we have seen that it was to cleanse us that Jesus gave himself.[7] Let Him, let God the Lord, cleanse you. Having these promises of a divine cleansing, cleanse yourselves. Believe that every sin, when it is forgiven you, is also cleansed away. It will be to you according to your faith. Let your faith in God, in the Word, in the blood, in Jesus increase continually: "God is faithful and just to cleanse us from all unrighteousness."

Lord God, I thank you for these promises. You have given not only forgiveness but also cleansing. As surely as forgiveness comes first, so does cleansing follow for everyone who desires it and who believes. Lord, let your Word penetrate my heart, and let a divine cleansing from every sin that is forgiven me be the stable expectation of my soul.

Beloved Savior, let the glorious, ceaseless cleansing of your blood through your Spirit in me be made known to me and shared by me every moment. Amen.

1. What is the connection between cleansing by God and cleansing by man himself?

2. What, according to 1 John 1:9, are the two things that must precede cleansing?

3. Is cleansing, as well as forgiveness, the work of God in us? If this is the case, of what inexpressible importance is it to trust God for it? (To believe that God gives me a divine cleansing in the blood when He forgives me is the way to become a partaker of it.)

4. What, according to Scripture, are the evidences of a pure heart?

5. What are "clean hands"? (Ps. 24).

---

[7]Eph. 5:26; Titus 2:14

CHAPTER 14

Holiness

"As he which hath called you is holy, so be ye holy in all manner of conversation; because it is written, Be ye holy; for I am holy" (1 Pet. 1:15, 16).

"But of him are ye in Christ Jesus, who of God is made unto us . . . sanctification" (1 Cor. 1:30).

"God hath from the beginning chosen you to salvation through sanctification of the Spirit and belief of the truth" (2 Thess. 2:13).

Not only salvation but holiness—salvation in holiness; for this purpose has God chosen and called us. Not only to be safe in Christ but holy in Christ must be the goal of the new believer. Safety and salvation are, in the long run, found only in holiness. The Christian who thinks that his salvation consists merely in safety and not in holiness will find himself deceived. New believer, listen to the Word of God: "Be ye holy."

And why must I be holy? Because He who called me is holy and summons me to fellowship and conformity with himself. How can anyone be saved in God when he has not the same disposition as God?[1]

God's holiness is His highest glory. In His holiness His righteousness and love are united. His holiness is the flaming fire of His zeal against all that is sin, whereby He keeps himself free from sin, and in love makes others also free from it. It is as the Holy One of Israel that He is the Redeemer,

---

[1]Ex. 19:6; Lev. 11:44; 19:2; 20:6, 7

58

and that He dwells in the midst of His people.[2] Redemption is given to bring us to himself and to the fellowship of His holiness. We cannot possibly share in the love and salvation of God if we are not holy as He is holy.[3] New believer, be holy.

And what is this holiness that I must have? Of God are you in Christ, who of God is made unto you sanctification. Christ is your sanctification; the life of Christ in you is your holiness.[4] In Christ you are sanctified; you are holy. In Christ you must still be sanctified; the glory of Christ must penetrate your whole life.

Holiness is more than purity. In Scripture we see that cleansing precedes holiness.[5] Cleansing is the taking away of that which is wrong—liberation from sin. Holiness is the filling with that which is good, divine, with the disposition of Jesus. Conformity to Him—this is holiness. Separation from the spirit of the world and being filled with the presence of the Holy God—this is holiness. The tabernacle was holy because God dwelt there; we are holy, as God's temple, after we have the indwelling of God. Christ's life in us is our holiness.[6]

And how do we become holy? By the sanctification of the Spirit. The Spirit of God is named the Holy Spirit because He makes us holy. He reveals and glorifies Christ in us. Through Him Christ dwells in us, and His holy power works in us. Through this Holy Spirit the workings of the flesh are mortified, and God works in us both the will and the accomplishment.[7]

And what is the work that we have to do to receive this holiness of Christ through the Holy Spirit? "God chose you . . . to salvation in sanctification of the Spirit *and belief of*

---

[2]Ex. 15:11; Isa. 12:6; 41:14; 43:15; 49:7; Hos. 11:9
[3]Isa. 10:17; Heb. 12:14
[4]1 Cor. 1:2; Eph. 5:27
[5]2 Cor. 7:1; Eph. 5:26, 27; 2 Tim. 2:21
[6]Ex. 29:43; 1 Cor. 1:2; 3:16, 17; 6:19
[7]Rom. 1:4; 8:2, 13; 1 Pet. 1:2

the truth.[8] The holiness of Christ becomes ours through faith.

There must first be the *desire* to become holy. We must cleanse ourselves from all pollutions of flesh and spirit by confessing them, giving them up to God, and having them cleansed away in the blood. Then, only, can we perfect holiness.[9]

Second, there must be *belief* of the truth that Christ himself is our sanctification; we have to receive from Him what is prepared in His fullness for us.[10] We must be deeply convinced that Christ is wholly and alone our sanctification as He is our justification, and that He will actually and powerfully work in us that which is well-pleasing to God. In this faith we must know that we have sufficient power for holiness and that our work is to receive this power from Him by faith every day.[11] He gives His Spirit, the Holy Spirit, in us; the Spirit communicates the holy life of Jesus to us.

New believer, the Three-One God is the Thrice-Holy.[12] And this Three-One God is the God that sanctifies you—the Father, by giving Jesus to you and confirming you in Jesus; the Son, by himself becoming your sanctification and giving you the Spirit; the Spirit by revealing the Son in you, preparing you as a temple for the indwelling of God, and making the Son dwell in you. Oh, be holy, for God is holy.

Lord God, the Holy One of Israel, what thanks shall I give to you for the gift of your Son as my sanctification and that I am sanctified in Him! And what thanks should I give for the Spirit of sanctification to dwell in me and transplant the holiness of Jesus into me! Lord, cause me to understand this truth and to long for the experience of it. Amen.

1. What is the distinction between forgiveness and

[8]2 Thess. 2:13
[9]2 Cor. 7:1
[10]John 1:14, 16; 1 Cor. 2:9, 10
[11]Gal. 2:21; Eph. 2:10; Phil. 2:13; 4:13
[12]Isa. 6:3; Rev. 4:8; 15:3, 4

cleansing, between cleansing and holiness?

2. What made the temple a sanctuary? The indwelling of God. What makes us holy? Nothing less than this: the indwelling of God in Christ by the Holy Spirit. Obedience and purity are the way to holiness; holiness itself is something higher.

3. In Isa. 57:17, there is a description of the man who will become holy. It is he who in poverty of spirit acknowledges that even when he is living as a righteous man, he has nothing and looks to God to come and dwell in him.

4. No one is holy but the Lord. You have as much of holiness as you have of God in you.

5. The word "holy" is one of the deepest words in the Bible, the deepest mystery of the Godhead. Do you desire to understand something of it and to obtain part in it? Then take these two thoughts, "I am holy," and "Be ye holy," and carry them in your heart as a seed of God that has life.

CHAPTER 15

Righteousness

"He hath showed thee, O man, what is good; and what doth the Lord require of thee, but to do justly, and to love mercy, and to walk humbly with thy God?" (Mic. 6:8).

"Yield yourselves unto God as those that are alive from the dead, and your members as instruments of righteousness unto God. Being then made free from sin, ye became the servants of righteousness. . . . Even so now yield your members servants to righteousness unto holiness" (Rom. 6:13, 18, 19).

The Word of Micah teaches us that the fruit of the salvation of God is seen chiefly in three things. The new life must be characterized in my relation to God and His will, by righteousness and doing right; in my relation to my neighbor, by love and kindness; in relation to myself, by humility and lowliness. For the present, let us meditate on righteousness.

Scripture teaches us that no man is righteous before God, or has any righteousness that can stand before God;[1] that man receives the rightness or righteousness of Christ as a free gift; and that by this righteousness, which is received in faith, he is then justified before God,[2] he is right with God. This righteous sentence of God is something effectual, whereby the life of righteousness is implanted in man, and he learns to live as a righteous man and to do righteousness.[3]

---

[1]Ps. 14:3; 143:2; Rom. 3:10, 20
[2]Rom. 3:22, 24; 10:3, 10; 1 Cor. 1:30; 2 Cor. 5:21; Gal. 2:16; Phil. 3:9
[3]Rom. 5:17, 18; 6:13, 18, 19; 8:3; Titus 1:3; 2:12; 1 John 2:29; 3:9, 10

62

Being right with God is followed by doing right. "The righteous shall live by faith" a righteous life.

It is to be feared that this is seldom understood. Most people think more on justification than on righteousness in life and walk. To understand the will and the thoughts of God, let us trace what Scripture teaches us on this point. We shall be persuaded that the man who is clothed with a divine righteousness before God must also walk before God and man in a divine righteousness.

Consider how, in the Word, the servants of God are praised as righteous,[4] how the favor and blessing of God are pronounced upon the righteous,[5] how the righteous are called to confidence and joy.[6] See this especially in the book of Psalms. See how in Proverbs, even though you were to take only one chapter, all blessing is pronounced upon the righteous.[7] See how everywhere men are divided into two classes— the righteous and the godless.[8] See how, in the New Testament, the Lord Jesus declares this righteousness;[9] how Paul, who announces most dearly the doctrine of justification by faith alone, insists that this is the aim of justification—to form righteous men who do right.[10] See how John names righteousness along with love as the two indispensable marks of the children of God.[11] When you put all these facts together, it must be very evident to you that a true Christian is one who does righteousness in all things, even as God is righteous.

And what this righteousness is Scripture will also teach you. It is a life in accordance with the commands of God in all their breadth and height. The righteous man does what

[4]Gen. 6:9; 7:1; Matt. 1:19; Luke 1:6; 2:25; 2 Pet. 2:7

[5]Ps. 1:6; 5:12; 14:5; 34:16, 20; 37:17, 39; 92:13; 97:11; 146:8

[6]Ps. 32:11; 33:1; 58:11; 64:10; 68:4; 97:12

[7]Prov. 10:3, 6, 7, 11, 16, 20, 21, 24, 25, 28, 30, 31, 32

[8]Eccles. 3:17; Isa. 3:10; Ezek. 3:18, 20; 18:21, 23; 33:12; Mal. 3:18; Matt. 5:45; 12:49; 25:46

[9]Matt. 5:6, 20; 6:33

[10]Rom. 3:31; 6:13, 22; 7:4, 6; 8:4; 2 Cor. 9:9, 10; Phil. 1:11; 1 Tim. 6:11

[11]1 John 2:4, 11, 29; 3:10; 5:2

is right in the eyes of the Lord.[12] He does not take the rules of human action; he does not ask what man considers lawful. As a man who stands right with God, he dreads above all things even the least unrighteousness. He is afraid, above all, of being partial to himself, of doing any wrong to his neighbor for the sake of his own advantage. In great and little things alike, he takes the Scripture as his measure and rule. As the ally of God, he knows that the way of righteousness is the way of blessing and life and joy.

Consider further the promises of blessing and joy which God has for the righteous, and then live as one who, in friendship with God and clothed with the righteousness of His Son through faith, has no alternative but to do righteousness.

O Lord, you have said, "There is no God else beside me: a just God and a Savior." You are my God. It is as a righteous God that you are my Savior and have redeemed me in your Son. As a righteous God you make me also righteous and say to me that the righteous shall live by faith. O Lord, let the new life in me be the life of faith, the life of a righteous man. Amen.

1. Observe the connection between the doing of righteousness and sanctification in Rom. 6:19, 22: "Present your members as servants to righteousness unto sanctification. . . . Having become servants to God, ye have your fruit unto sanctification." The doing of righteousness, righteousness in conduct and action, is the way to holiness. Obedience is the way to become filled with the Holy Spirit. And the indwelling of God through the Spirit—this is holiness.

2. "Suffer it now: for thus it becometh us to fulfill all righteousness." It was when the Lord Jesus had spoken that word that He was baptized with the Spirit. Let us set aside every temptation not to walk in full obedience to God, even as He did, and we too shall be filled with the Spirit. "Blessed are they that do hunger and thirst after righteousness."

3. Take pains to set before yourselves the image of a man

---

[12]Ps. 119:166, 168; Luke 1:6, 75; 1 Thess. 2:10

who so walks that the name "righteous" is involuntarily given to him. Think of his uprightness, his conscientious care to cause no one to suffer the least injury, his holy fear and carefulness to transgress none of the commands of the Lord— righteous, and walking in all the commandments and ordinances of the Lord blameless; and then say to the Lord that you should so live.

4. You understand now the great word, "The righteous shall live by faith." By faith the godless is justified and becomes a righteous man; by faith he lives as a righteous man.

CHAPTER 16

Love

"A new commandment I give unto you, That ye love one another; as I have loved you, that ye also love one another. By this shall all men know that ye are my disciples, if ye have love one to another" (John 13:34, 35).

"Love worketh no ill to his neighbour: therefore love is the fulfilling of the law" (Rom. 13:10).

"Beloved, if God so loved us, we ought also to love one another. If we love one another, God dwelleth in us, and his love is perfected in us" (1 John 4:11, 12).

In the word of Micah, in the previous section, righteousness was the first thing and to love mercy the second thing that God demands. Righteousness stood more in the foreground in the Old Testament. It is in the New Testament that we first see that love is supreme. Declarations to this effect are not difficult to find. It is in the coming of Jesus that the love of God is fully revealed; that the new, the eternal life, is fully given; that we become children of the Father and brethren of one another.

On this basis the Lord can then, for the first time, speak of the new commandment—the commandment of brotherly love. Righteousness is required as much in the New Testament as in the Old.[1] Yet the burden of the New Testament is that power has been given us for a love that in early days was impossible.[2]

---

[1]Matt. 5:6, 17, 20; 6:33
[2]John 13:34; Rom. 5:5; Gal. 5:22; 1 Thess. 4:9; 1 John 4:11

66

Let every Christian take it deeply to heart that in the first and the great commandment—the new commandment given by Jesus at His departure—the peculiar characteristic of a disciple of Jesus is brotherly love. And let him with his whole heart yield himself to Christ to obey that command. For the proper exercise of this brotherly love, one must take heed to more than one thing.

Love to the brethren flows from the love of the Father. By the Holy Spirit, the love of God is shed abroad in our hearts; the wonderful love of the Father is unveiled to us so that His love becomes the life and joy of our soul. Out of this fountain of His love for us springs our love to Him.[3] And our love to Him naturally works love to the brethren.[4]

Do not, then, attempt to fulfill the commandment of brotherly love by yourself; you are not in a position to do this. But believe that the Holy Spirit, who is in you to make known the love of God, will enable you to yield this love. Never say, "I feel no love. I do not feel as if I can forgive this man." Feeling is not the rule of your duty, but the command and the faith that God gives power to obey the command.

In obedience to the Father, with the choice of your will, and in faith that the Holy Spirit gives you power, begin to say, "I will love him. I do love him." The feeling will follow the faith. Grace gives power for all that the Father asks of you.[5]

Brotherly love has its measure and rule in the love of Jesus. "This is my commandment, that ye love one another, as I have loved you." [6] The eternal life that works in us is the life of Jesus. It knows no other law than what we see in Him. It works with power in us what it worked through Him. Jesus himself lives in us and loves in and through us; we must believe in the power of this love in us, and in that faith love as He loved. Oh, do believe that this is true salvation—to love even as Jesus loves.

[3]Rom. 5:5; 1 John 4:19
[4]Eph. 4:2, 6; 5:1, 2; 1 John 3:1; 4:7, 20; 5:1
[5]Matt. 5:44, 45; Gal. 2:20; 1 Thess. 3:12, 13; 5:24; Phil. 4:13; 1 Pet. 1:22
[6]Luke 22:26, 27; John 13:14, 15, 34; Col. 2:13

Brotherly love must be in deed and in truth.[7] It is not mere feeling; faith working by love is what has power in Christ. It manifests itself in all the characteristics that are enumerated in the Word of God. Contemplate its glorious image in 1 Cor. 13:4–7. Mark all the glorious encouragements to gentleness, to long-suffering, to mercy.[8] In all your conduct, let it be seen that the love of Christ dwells in you. Let your love be a helpful, self-sacrificing love—like that of Jesus. Hold all children of God, however frail and failing they may be, fervently dear. Let love to them teach you to love all men.[9] Let your household, and the church, and the world see in you one with whom "love is greatest"; one in whom the love of God has a full dwelling, a free working.

God is love. Jesus is the gift of this love, to bring love to you, to transplant you into that life of Godlike love. Live in that faith and you shall not complain that you have no power to love; the love of the Spirit shall be your power and your life.

Beloved Savior, I see more clearly that the whole of the new life is a life in love. You are the Son of God's love, the gift of His love, come to introduce us into His love and to give us a dwelling there. And the Holy Spirit is given to shed abroad the love of God in our hearts, to open a spring out of which shall stream love to you and to the brethren and to all mankind. Lord, here am I, one redeemed by love, to live for it, and in its power to love all. Amen.

1. Those who reject the Word of God sometimes say that it is of no importance what we believe if we but have love, and so they want to make love the one condition of salvation. In their zeal against this view, the orthodox party have sometimes presented faith in justification as if love were not of

---

[7]Matt. 12:50; 25:40; Rom. 13:10; 1 Cor. 7:19; Gal. 5:6; James 2:15, 16; 1 John 3:16, 17, 18

[8]Gal. 5:22; Eph. 4:2, 32; Phil. 2:2, 3; Col. 3:12; 2 Thess. 1:3

[9]Luke 6:32, 35; 1 Pet. 1:22; 2 Pet. 1:7

such importance. This is likely to be very dangerous. God is love. His Son is the gift—the bringer—of His love to us. The Spirit sheds abroad the love of God in the heart. The new life is a life in love. Love is the greatest thing. Let it be the chief element in our life—namely, true love, which is known in the keeping of God's commandments. (See 1 John 3:10, 23, 24; 5:2.)

2. Do not wonder that I have said to you that you must love even though you do not feel the least love. It is not what you feel but what you will that is your power. It is not in your feeling but in faith that the Spirit in you is the power of your will to work in you all that the Father asks you. Therefore, although you feel absolutely no love toward your enemy, say in the obedience of faith, "Father, I love him; in faith in the hidden working of the Spirit in my heart, I do love him."

3. Do not think that this is love if you merely wish no evil toward anyone, or if you should be willing to help if he were in need. No, love is much more; love is the disposition with which God addressed you when you were His enemy, and afterward ran to you with tender longing to bless you.

CHAPTER 17

Humility

"And what doth the Lord require of thee, but to do justly, and to love mercy, and to walk humbly with thy God?" (Mic. 6:8).

"Learn of me; for I am meek and lowly in heart: and ye shall find rest unto your souls" (Matt. 11:29)

One of the most dangerous enemies of the new believer is pride, or self-exaltation. There is no sin that works more cunningly and more hiddenly. It knows how to penetrate into everything, even into our service for God, our prayers, even into our humility. There is nothing so small in the earthly life, nothing so holy in the spiritual life, out of which self-exaltation does not know how to extract its nutriment.[1] The believer must therefore be on his guard against it, must listen to what Scripture teaches about it and about the lowliness whereby it is driven out.

Man was created to share in the glory of God. He obtains this by surrendering himself to the glorification of God. The more he seeks that only the glory of God shall be seen in him, the more this glory rests upon himself.[2] The more he forgets and loses himself, desiring to be nothing in order that God may be all and be alone glorified, the happier he will be.

By sin, this design has been thwarted; man seeks himself

---

[1] 2 Chron. 26:5, 16; 32:26, 31; Isa. 65:5; Jer. 7:4; 2 Cor. 12:7

[2] Isa. 43:7, 21; John 12:28; 13:31; 32; 17:1, 4, 5; 1 Cor. 10:31; 2 Thess. 1:11, 12

and his own will.[3] Grace has come to restore what sin has corrupted, and to bring man to glory by the pathway of dying unto himself and living solely for the glory of God. This is the humility or lowliness of which Jesus is the model: He took no thought for himself; He gave himself over wholly to glorify the Father.[4]

He who would be freed from self-exaltation must not think to obtain this by striving against its mere workings. No, pride must be driven out and kept out by humility. The Spirit of life in Christ, the Spirit of His lowliness, will work in us true lowliness.[5]

The means that He will chiefly use for this purpose is the Word. It is by the Word that we are cleansed from sin; it is by the Word that we are sanctified and filled with the love of God.

Observe what the Word says about this. It speaks of God's hatred toward pride and the punishment that comes upon it.[6] It gives the most glorious promises to the lowly.[7] In nearly every epistle, humility is commended to Christians as one of the first virtues.[8] It is the feature in the image of Jesus which He seeks chiefly to impress on His disciples. His whole incarnation and redemption has its roots in His humiliation.[9]

Take some of these words of God from time to time and treasure them in your heart. The tree of life yields many different kinds of seed—the seed also of the heavenly plant, lowliness. The seeds are the words of God. Carry them in your heart; they shall shoot up and yield fruit.[10]

Consider, moreover, how lovely, how becoming, how well-pleasing to God lowliness is. As man, created for the honor

---

[3]Rom. 1:21, 23
[4]John 8:50; Phil. 2:7
[5]Rom. 8:2; Phil. 2:5
[6]Ps. 31:23; Prov. 16:5; Matt. 23:12; Luke 1:51; James 4:6; 1 Pet. 5:5
[7]Ps. 34:19; Prov. 11:2; Isa. 57:15; Luke 9:48; 14:11; 18:14
[8]Rom. 12:3, 16; 1 Cor. 13:4; Gal. 5:22, 23, 26; Eph. 4:2; Phil. 2:3
[9]Matt. 20:26, 28; Luke 22:27; John 13:14, 15; Phil. 2:7, 8
[10]1 Thess. 2:13; Heb. 4:12; James 1:21

of God, you find humility natural to you.[11] As a sinner, deeply unworthy, you have nothing more to urge against it.[12] As a redeemed soul, who knows that only through the death of the natural "I" does the way to the new life lie, you find it indispensable.[13] As a child of the Father, overwhelmed with His love, you must consider it above all else.[14]

But here, as everywhere in the life of grace, let faith be the chief element. Believe in the power of the eternal life that works in you. Believe in the power of Jesus who is your life. Believe in the power of the Holy Spirit who dwells in you.

Do not attempt to hide your pride, or to forget it, or to root it out yourself. Confess this sin, with every working of it that you trace, in the sure confidence that the blood cleanses, that the Spirit sanctifies.

Learn of Jesus that He is meek and lowly in heart. Consider that He is your life with all that He has. Believe that He gives His humility to you. The words "Do it to the Lord Jesus" mean, "Be clothed with the Lord Jesus." Be clothed with humility in order that you may be clothed with Jesus. It is Christ in you who shall fill you with humility.

Blessed Lord Jesus, there never was anyone among the children of men so high, so holy, so glorious as you are. And never was there anyone who was so lowly and ready to deny himself as the servant of all. O Lord, when shall we learn that lowliness is the grace by which man can be most closely conformed to the divine glory? Oh, teach me this! Amen.

1. Take heed that you do nothing to feed the pride of others. Take heed that you do not allow others to feed your pride. Take heed, above all, that you do nothing yourself to feed your pride. Let God alone always and in all things obtain

---

[11]Gen. 1:27; 1 Cor. 11:7
[12]Job 42:6; Isa. 6:5; Luke 5:8
[13]Rom. 7:18; 1 Cor. 15:9, 10; Gal. 2:20
[14]Gen. 32:10; 2 Sam. 7:18; 1 Pet. 5:6–10

the honor. Endeavor to observe all that is good in His children and to thank Him heartily for it. Thank Him for all that helps you to hold yourself in small esteem, whether it be sent through friend or foe. Determine never on any account to be eager for your own honor. Commit this to the Father. Take heed only to His honor.

2. Do not think that faintheartedness or doubting is lowliness. Deep humility and strong faith go together. The centurion who said, "I am not worthy that thou shouldst come under my roof," and the woman who said, "Yea, Lord, yet even the dogs eat of the crumbs"—these two were the most humble and the most trustful that the Lord found (see Matt. 8:10; 15:28). The reason is this: The nearer we are to God, the less we are in ourselves and the stronger we are in Him. The more I see of God, the less I become and the deeper is my confidence in Him. To become lowly, let God fill your eyes and heart. Where God is all, there is no time or place for ourselves.

CHAPTER 18

Stumblings

"In many things we offend [stumble] all" (James 3:2).

This word of God through James is the description of what the Christian is when he is not kept by grace. It serves to take away from us all hope in ourselves.[1] "Now unto him that is able to keep you from falling . . . be glory and majesty, dominion and power, both now and ever" (Jude 24, 25).

This word of God in Jude points to Him who can keep from falling and stirs up the soul to ascribe to Him the honor and the power. It serves to confirm our hope in God.[2]

"Brethren, give diligence to make your calling and election sure: for if ye do these things, ye shall never fall" (2 Pet. 1:10). This word of God through Peter teaches us the way in which we can become partakers of the keeping power of the Almighty—the confirmation of our election by God in a God-like walk (vv. 4, 8, 11). It serves to lead us into diligence and conscientious watchfulness.[3]

For the new believer, it is often a difficult question as to what he ought to think of his stumblings. On this point he ought especially to be on his guard against two errors. Some become discouraged when they stumble; they think their surrender was not sincere and so lose their confidence toward God.[4] Others take it too lightly; they think that it is normal.

---

[1]Rom. 7:14, 23; Gal. 6:1
[2]2 Cor. 1:9; 1 Thess. 5:24; 2 Thess. 2:16, 17; 3:3
[3]Matt. 26:41; Luke 12:35; 1 Pet. 1:13; 5:8–10
[4]Heb. 3:6, 14; 10:35

They show little concern about their stumblings and continue to live in them.[5] Let us permit these words of God to teach us what we ought to think of our stumblings. There are three lessons.

Let not stumblings discourage you. You are called to perfectness; yet this does not come at once. Time and patience are needful for it. Therefore James says, "Let patience have its perfect work, that ye may be perfect and entire."[6] Do not think that your surrender was not sincere; acknowledge only how weak you still are. And do not believe that you must continue stumbling; acknowledge only how strong your Savior is.

Let stumbling rouse you to faith in the mighty keeper. You have stumbled because you have not relied on Him with a sufficient faith.[7] Let stumbling drive you to Him. The first thing you must do with a stumbling is to go with it to Jesus. Tell Him of your stumbling.[8] Confess it and receive forgiveness. Confess it and commit yourself with your weakness to Him, counting on Him to keep you. Sing continually the song, "To Him that is mighty to keep you, be the glory."

Let stumbling make you very wise.[9] By faith you shall strive and overcome. In the power of your keeper and the joy and security of His help, you shall have courage to stand. The firmer you confirm your election, the more conscientious you will live in all things only for Him, in Him, and through Him.[10] Doing this, the Word of God says you will never stumble.

Lord Jesus, stumbling and falling do not bring glory to your name. You are mighty to keep me from stumbling. Yours is the might and the power. I take you as my keeper. I look to

---

[5]Rom. 6:1; Gal. 2:18; 3:3

[6]Matt. 5:48; 2 Tim. 3:17; Heb. 13:20, 21; James 1:4; 1 Pet. 5:10

[7]Matt. 14:31; 17:20

[8]Ps. 38:18; 69:6; 1 John 1:9; 2:1

[9]Prov. 28:14; Phil. 2:12; 1 Pet. 1:17, 18

[10]2 Chron. 20:15; Ps. 18:30, 37; 44:5, 9; John 5:4, 5; Rom. 11:20; 2 Cor. 1:24; Phil. 2:13

your love which has chosen me, and wait for the fulfillment of your Word, "Ye shall never stumble." Amen.

1. Let your thoughts about what the grace of God can do for you be taken only from the Word of God. Our natural expectations—that we must always be stumbling—are lies. They are strengthened by more than one thing. There is secret unwillingness to surrender everything. There is the example of so many sluggish Christians. There is the unbelief that cannot quite understand that God will really keep us. There is the experience of so many disappointments when we have striven in our own power.

2. Let no stumbling be tolerated because it seems unimportant.

CHAPTER 19

Jesus the Keeper

"The Lord is thy keeper. . . . The Lord shall preserve thee from all evil: he shall preserve thy soul" (Ps. 121:5, 7).

"I know whom I have believed, and am persuaded that he is able to keep that which I have committed unto him against that day" (2 Tim. 1:12).

For new believers who are still weak, there is no lesson that is more necessary than this: the Lord has not only received them, but He will also keep them.[1] The lovely name "the Lord thy keeper" must be carried in the heart until the assurance of an Almighty keeping becomes as strong with us as it was with Paul when he wrote these glorious words: "I know whom I have believed, and am persuaded that he is able to keep that which I have committed unto him against that day." Come and learn this lesson from him.

Learn from Jesus to deposit your pledge, or commitment, with Him. Paul had surrendered himself—body and soul—to the Lord Jesus; that was his pledge which he had deposited with the Lord.

You also have surrendered yourselves to the Lord, but perhaps not with the clear understanding that it needs to be *kept* every day. Do this daily. Deposit your soul with Jesus as a costly pledge that He will keep secure. Do this same thing with every part of your life.

Is there something that you cannot seem to hold? Your

---

[1]Gen. 28:15; Deut. 7:9; 32:10; Ps. 17:8; 89:33, 34; Rom. 11:2, 29

heart, because it is too worldly?[2] your tongue, because it is too idle?[3] your temper, because it is too passionate?[4] your calling to confess the Lord, because you are too weak?[5] Learn, then, to deposit it as a commitment for keeping with Jesus in order that He may fulfill in you the promise of God about it.

You often pray and strive in vain against a sin; it is because you would be the person who would overcome. No, entrust the matter wholly to Jesus. "The battle is not yours, but God's."[6] Leave it in His hands. Believe in Him to do it for you. "This is the victory that hath overcome the world, even your faith."[7] But you must first remove it wholly out of your hands and place it into His.

Learn from Paul to set your confidence *only in the power of Jesus*. I am persuaded that *He is able* to keep my commitment. You have an almighty Jesus to keep you. Faith keeps itself occupied only with His power.[8] Let your faith be strengthened in what God is able to do for you.[9] Expect with certainty that He will do for you great and glorious things entirely above your own strength. See in the Scriptures how constantly the power of God was the ground of the trust of His people. Take these words and hide them in your heart. Let the power of Jesus fill your soul. Ask only, "What is my Jesus able to do?" What you really trust Him with He is able to keep.[10]

Learn also from Paul where he obtained the assurance that this power would keep what he had committed to Him. It was *in his knowledge of Jesus*. "I know whom I have be-

[2]Ps. 51:17; Jer. 31:33

[3]Ps. 31:6; 141:3

[4]Ps. 119:165; Jer. 26:3, 4; John 14:27; Phil. 4.6, 7; 2 Thess. 3·16

[5]Isa. 1:7; Jer. 1:9; Matt. 10:19, 20

[6]Ex. 14:14; Deut. 3:22; 20:4; 2 Chron. 20:15

[7]Matt. 9:28; 1 John 5:3, 4

[8]Gen. 17:1; 18:14; Jer. 32:17, 27; Matt. 8:27; 28:18; Luke 1:37, 49; 18:27; Rom. 4:21; Heb. 11:19

[9]Rom. 4:21; 14:4; 2 Cor. 9:8; 2 Tim. 1:13

[10]John 13:1; 1 Cor. 1:8, 9

78

lieved"; therefore I am assured.[11] You can trust the power of Jesus if you *know* that He is yours, if you hold conversation with Him as your friend. Then you can say, "I know whom I have believed. I know that He holds me very dear. I know and am assured that He is able to keep my pledge."

This is the way to the full assurance of faith. Deposit your pledge with Jesus; give yourself wholly—give everything—into His hands; let your thoughts dwell on His power and depend upon Him; and live with Him so that you may always know who He is and whom you have believed.

New believers, receive this word: "The Lord is thy keeper." For every weakness, every temptation, learn to deposit your soul with Him as a pledge. You can depend upon it, you can shout joyfully over it: "The Lord shall keep you from all evil."[12]

Holy Jesus, I take you as my keeper. Let your name "The Lord your keeper" sound as a song in my heart the whole day. Teach me in every need to deposit my case as a pledge with you and to be assured that you are able to keep it. Amen.

1. There was a woman who for many years and with much prayer had battled her temper, but had not obtained the victory. On a certain day she resolved not to come out of her room until by earnest prayer she had the power to overcome. She came out in the opinion that she would succeed. She had hardly been in the household when something gave her offense and caused her to be angry. She was deeply ashamed, burst into tears, and hurried back to her room. A daughter, who understood the way of faith better than she, went to her and said, "Mother, I have observed your conflict; may I tell you what I think the hindrance is?"

"Yes, my child."

"Mother, you struggle against temper and pray that the Lord will help you to overcome. This is wrong. The Lord must do it alone. You must give your temper wholly into His hands;

---

[11]John 10:14, 28; Gal. 2:20; 2 Tim. 4:18; 1 John 2:13, 14
[12]Josh. 1:9; Ps. 23:4; Rom. 8:35

then He takes it wholly and He keeps you."

The mother could not understand this at first, but later it was made plain to her. And she enjoyed the blessedness of the life in which Jesus keeps us and we by faith have the victory. Do you understand this?

2. "The Lord must help us to overcome sin"; this expression is altogether outside of the New Testament. The grace of God in the soul does not come to help us. He will do everything: "The Spirit has made me free from the law of sin."

3. When you surrender anything to the Lord for keeping, take heed to two things: that you give it wholly into His hands; and that you leave it there. Let Him have it wholly. He will fulfill your deepest desire.

CHAPTER 20

Power in Weakness

"He said unto me, My grace is sufficient for thee: for my strength is made perfect in weakness. Most gladly therefore will I rather glory in my infirmities, that the power of Christ may rest upon me. Therefore I take pleasure in infirmities . . . for when I am weak, then am I strong" (2 Cor. 12:9, 10).

There is almost no word that is so imperfectly understood in the Christian life as the word *weakness*. Sin and shortcoming, sluggishness and disobedience, are said to be on account of our weakness. With this appeal to weakness, the true sense of guilt and the sincere endeavor after progress are impossible.

Should I feel guilty when I do not do what God has not empowered me to do? The Father does not demand of His child what He has not made provision for. The Father under the New Covenant does not do that. He requires of us nothing more than what He has given us power to do in His Holy Spirit. The new life is a life in the power of Christ through the Spirit.

The error of this mode of thinking is that people estimate their weakness not too highly but too moderately. They would still do something by the exercise of all their powers and with the help of God. They do not see that they must be nothing before God.[1] You think that you still have a little strength and that the Father must help you by adding something of His own power to your feeble energy. This thought

---

[1] Rom. 4:4, 5; 11:6; 1 Cor. 1:27, 28

is wrong. Your weakness appears in the fact that *you can do nothing*. It is better to speak of utter inability; that is what the Scriptures understand by the word "weakness." "Apart from me, ye can do nothing." "In us is no power."[2]

Whenever the new believer acknowledges his weakness, then he learns to understand the secret of the power of Jesus. He then sees that he is not to wait and pray to become stronger, to feel stronger. No, in his inability he is to have the power of Jesus. By faith he is to receive it; he is to reckon that it is for him and that Jesus himself will work in and by him.[3]

It then becomes clear to him the meaning of the Lord's words, "My strength is made perfect in [your] weakness." He knows the answer is, "When I am weak, then am I strong." Yea, the weaker I am, the stronger I become. And he learns to sing with Paul, "I take pleasure in weaknesses." "We rejoice when we are weak."[4]

It is wonderful how glorious the life of faith becomes for him who is content to have nothing or feel nothing in himself and always lives in the power of his Lord. He learns to understand what a joyful thing it is to know God as his strength. "The Lord is my strength and song."[5] He lives in what the Psalms so often express: "I love thee, O Lord, my strength"; "I will sing of thy strength: unto thee, O my strength, will I sing praises."[6] He understands what is meant when a psalm says, "Give strength to the Lord: the Lord will give strength to his people"; and when another says, "Give strength to God: the God of Israel, he giveth strength and power to his people."[7] When we give or ascribe all the power to God, then He gives it to us again.

"I have written unto you, young men, because ye are strong, and the word of God abideth in you, and ye have

---

[2] 2 Chron. 16:9; 20:12; John 5:19; 15:5; 2 Cor. 1:9

[3] John 15:5; 1 Cor. 1:24; 15:10; Eph. 1:18, 19; Col. 1:11

[4] 2 Cor. 11:30; 12:9, 11; 13:4, 9

[5] Ps. 89:13; 118:14

[6] Ps. 18:2; 28:7, 8; 31:4; 43:2; 46:1; 59:17; 62:7; 81:2

[7] Ps. 29:1, 11; 68:35

overcome the wicked one." The Christian is strong in his Lord[8]—not sometimes strong and sometimes weak but always weak and therefore always strong. He has simply to know and use his strength trustfully. To be strong is a command, a word that must be obeyed. From obedience there comes more strength. "Be strong . . . and he shall strengthen thine heart." In faith the Christian must simply obey the command, "Be strong in the Lord, and in the power of his might."[9]

The God of the Lord Jesus, the Father of glory, give unto us the spirit of wisdom and of revelation in the knowledge of Jesus that we may know what is the exceeding greatness of His power to us who believe. Amen.

1. As long as the Christian thinks of the service of God or of sanctification as something that is hard and difficult, he will make no progress in it. He must see that this very thing is impossible for him. Then he will cease endeavoring to do something; he will surrender himself that Christ may work all in him.

2. The complaint about weakness is often nothing other than an apology for our idleness. There is power to be obtained in Christ for those who will take the pains to have it.

3. "Be strong in the Lord, and in the power of his might." Obey that. I must abide *in the Lord* and in the power of *His might*; then I become strong. To have His power I must have himself. The strength is His and continues His; the weakness continues mine. He, the strong, works in me, the weak; I, the weak, abide by faith in Him, the strong. And I, in the selfsame moment, know myself to be weak and strong.

4. Strength is for work. He who would be strong simply to be holy will not be so. He who in his weakness begins to work for the Lord shall become strong.

---

[8]Ps. 71:16; 1 John 2:14
[9]Ps. 27:14; 31:24; Isa. 40:31; Eph. 6:10

CHAPTER 21

The Life of Feeling

"We walk by faith, not by sight" (2 Cor. 5:7).
"Blessed are they that have not seen, and yet have believed"
(John 20:29).
"Said I not unto thee, that, if thou wouldest believe, thou shouldest see the glory of God?" (John 11:40).

In connection with your conversion there was no greater hindrance in your way than feeling. You thought, perhaps for years, that you must experience something, must feel and perceive something in yourselves. It seemed too hazardous to simply and without some feeling believe in the Word that God had received you and that your sins were forgiven. But at last you acknowledged that the way of faith, without feeling, was the way of the Word of God. And it has been to you the way of salvation. Through faith alone have you been saved, and your soul has found rest and peace.[1]

In the Christian life there is no temptation that is more persistent and more dangerous than this same feeling. The word "feeling" is not found in Scripture. What we call "feeling" the Scripture calls "seeing." It tells us repeatedly that not seeing but believing—believing in opposition to what we see—gives salvation. "[Abraham], being not weak in faith, he considered not his own body." Faith holds simply to what God says. The unbelief that would see shall not see; the faith that will not see, but has enough in God, shall see the glory

---

[1]John 3:36; Rom. 3:28; 4:5, 16; 5:1

84

of God.[2] The man who seeks for feeling and mourns about it shall not find it; the man who cares not for it shall have it overflowing. "Whosoever would save his life shall lose it, and whosoever shall lose his life for my sake shall find it." Later on, faith in the Word becomes sealed with true feeling by the Holy Spirit.[3]

New believer, learn to live by faith. Let it be maintained that faith is God's way to a blessed life. When there is no feeling of God's presence in prayer, when you feel cold and dull in the spirit, live by faith. Let your faith look upon Jesus as near, upon His power and faithfulness; and, though you have nothing to bring Him, believe that He will give you all. Feeling always seeks something in itself; faith keeps itself occupied with who Jesus is.[4]

When you read the Word and have no feeling of interest or blessing, read it yet again in faith. The Word will work and bring blessing; "the word worketh in those that believe." When you feel no love, believe in the love of Jesus and say in faith that He knows that you still love Him. When you have no feeling of gladness, believe in the inexpressible joy that there is in Jesus for you. Faith is blessedness and will give joy to those who are not concerned about the self-sufficiency that springs from joy but about the glorification of God that springs from faith.[5] Jesus will surely fulfill His word: "Blessed are they that have not seen, and yet have believed." "Said I not unto thee, that, if thou wouldest believe, thou shouldest see the glory of God?"

It is between the life of feeling and the life of faith that the Christian has to choose daily. Happy is he who, once for all, has made the firm choice and every morning renews the choice not to seek or listen for feeling but only to walk by faith according to the will of God. The faith that keeps itself occupied with the Word, with what God has said and, through

---

[2] 2 Chron. 7:2; Ps. 27:13; Isa. 7:9; Matt. 14:30, 31; Luke 5:5
[3] John 12:25; Gal. 3:2, 14; Eph. 1:13
[4] Rom. 4:20, 21; 2 Tim. 1:12; Heb. 11:5, 6; James 5:15, 16
[5] Rom. 15:13; Gal. 2:20; 1 Pet. 1:5, 7, 8

the Word, with God himself and Jesus His Son, shall taste the blessedness of a life in God above. Feeling seeks and aims at itself; faith honors God and shall be honored by Him. Faith pleases God and shall receive from Him the witness in the heart of the believer that he is acceptable to God.

Lord God, the one, the only, thing that you desire from your children is that they should trust you, and that they should always be in fellowship with you in that faith. Lord, let it be the one thing in which I seek my happiness—to honor and to please you by a faith that firmly holds you, the Invisible, and trusts you in all things. Amen.

1. There is something marvelous in the new life. It is difficult to make it clear to the new believer. The Spirit of God teaches him to understand it after he maintains a life of grace. Jesus has laid the foundation of that life in the first word of the Sermon on the Mount: "Blessed are the poor in spirit, for theirs is the kingdom of heaven." A feeling of deep poverty and of royal riches, of utter weakness and of kingly might, exist together in the soul. *To have nothing in itself, to have all in Christ*—that is the secret of faith. And the true secret of faith is to bring this into exercise, and in hours of barrenness and emptiness still to know that we have all in Christ.

2. Do not forget that the faith of which God's Word speaks so much stands not only in opposition to *works* but also in opposition to *feelings*, and therefore for a pure life of faith you must cease to seek your salvation not only in works but also in feelings. Let faith always speak against feeling. When feeling says, "In myself I am sinful, I am dark, I am weak, I am poor, I am sad," let faith say, "In Christ I am holy, I am light, I am strong, I am rich, I am joyful."

CHAPTER 22

The Holy Ghost

"And because ye are sons, God hath sent forth the Spirit of his Son into your hearts, crying, Abba, Father" (Gal. 4:6).

The great gift of the Father, through whom He obtained salvation and brought it near to us, is the Son. On the other hand, the great gift of the Son, whom He sends to us from the Father to apply to us an inner and effectual salvation, is the Holy Spirit.[1] As the Son reveals and glorifies the Father, so the Spirit reveals and glorifies the Son.[2] The Spirit is in us to transfer to us the life and the salvation that are prepared in Jesus, and He makes them wholly ours.[3] Jesus who is in heaven is made present in us—dwells in us—by the Spirit.

We have seen that in order to become partakers of Jesus there are always two things necessary: the knowledge of the sin that is in us and of the redemption that is in Him. It is the Holy Spirit who continually promotes this double work in believers. He reproves and comforts, He convinces of sin and He glorifies Christ.[4]

The Spirit convinces of sin. He is the light and the fire of God through whom sin is unveiled and consumed. He is the spirit of judgment and of burning by whom God purifies His people.[5]

---

[1] John 7:39; 14:16, 26; Acts 1:4, 5; 2:33; 1 Cor. 3:16
[2] John 15:26; 16:14, 15; 1 Cor. 2:10, 12; 12:3
[3] John 14:17, 26; Rom. 8:2; Eph. 3:17, 19
[4] John 16:9, 14
[5] Isa. 4:4; Zech. 12:10, 11; Matt. 3:11, 12

To the troubled person who complains that he does not feel his sin deeply enough, we must often say that there is no limit as to how deep his repentance must be. He must come daily just as he is; the deepest conviction oftentimes comes after conversion.

To the new believer we have simply to say: let the Spirit who is in you convince you of sin. Sin, which formerly you knew but by name, He will make you hate. Sin, which you had not seen in the hidden depth of your heart, He will make you know and with shame confess. Sin, of which you may have thought that you were free and which you had judged severely in others, He will point out to you in yourself.[6] And He will teach you with repentance to cast yourself entirely upon grace in order to be thereby redeemed and purified from it.

Beloved believer, the Holy Spirit is in you as the light and fire of God to unveil and to consume sin. The temple of God is holy, and this temple you are. Let the Holy Spirit in you have full mastery to point out and expel sin.[7] After He makes you know sin, He will at every point make you know Jesus as your life and your sanctification.

And then the Spirit who rebukes shall also comfort. He will glorify Jesus in you and take what is in Jesus and make it known to you. He will give you knowledge concerning the power of Jesus' blood to cleanse,[8] and the power of Jesus' indwelling to keep.[9] He will make you see how literally, how completely, how certainly Jesus is with you every moment to do His own work in you.

In the Holy Spirit, the living, almighty, and ever-present Jesus shall be your portion; you will know this and will have the full enjoyment of it. The Holy Spirit will teach you to bring all your sin and sinfulness to Jesus, and to know Jesus with His complete redemption from sin as your own. As the

---

[6]Ps. 139:7, 23; Isa. 10:17; Matt. 7:5; Rom. 14:4; 1 Cor. 2:10; 14:24, 25
[7]Ps. 19:13; 139:23; Mic. 3:8; 1 Cor. 3:17; 2 Cor. 3:17; 6:16
[8]1 John 1:7, 9
[9]Eph. 3:17–20; 1 Pet. 1:5

Spirit of sanctification, He will drive out sin in order that He may cause Jesus to dwell in you.[10]

Beloved new believer, take time to understand and to become filled with the truth: *the Holy Spirit is in you.* Review all the assurances of God's Word that this is so.[11] Never think of living as a Christian without the indwelling of the Spirit. Take pains to have your heart filled with the faith that the Spirit dwells in you and will do His mighty work, for through faith the Spirit comes and works.[12] Have a great reverence for the work of the Spirit in you. Seek Him daily to believe, to obey, to trust, and He will take and make known to you all that there is in Jesus. He will make Jesus very glorious to you and in you.

O my Father, I thank you for this gift which Jesus sent me from you. I thank you that I am now the temple of your Spirit and that He dwells in me.

Lord, teach me to believe this with my whole heart and to live in the world as one who knows that the Spirit of God is in him to lead him. Teach me to think with deep reverence and awe on this: God is in me. Lord, in that faith I have the power to be holy.

Holy Spirit, reveal to me all that sin is in me. Holy Spirit, reveal to me all that Jesus is in me. Amen.

1. Remember: the knowledge of the person and the work of the Holy Spirit is just as important as the knowledge of the person and the work of Christ.

2. Concerning the Holy Spirit, we must endeavor to hold fast the truth that He is given as the *fruit* of the work of Jesus for us, that He is the *power* of the life of Jesus in us, and that through Him, *Jesus himself* with His full salvation dwells in us.

3. In order to enjoy all this, we must be filled with the

[10]Rom. 1:4; 8:2, 13; 1 Pet. 1:2
[11]Rom. 8:14, 16; 1 Cor. 6:19; 2 Cor. 1:22; 6:16; Eph. 1:13
[12]Gal. 3:2, 5, 14; 5:5

Spirit. This simply means to be emptied of all else and full of Jesus. To deny ourselves, to take up the cross, to follow Jesus—this is the way to be filled with the Spirit of Jesus; or, rather, this is the way in which the Spirit leads us to His fullness. No one but he who is led by the Spirit has the power to enter fully into the death of Jesus. The one who desires this fullness, Jesus takes by the hand and brings in.

4. As the whole of salvation—the whole of the new life— is by faith, so is this also true of the gift and the working of the Holy Spirit. By faith, not by works nor by feeling, do I receive Him, am I led by Him, am I filled with Him.

5. As clear and definite as my faith is in the work that Jesus accomplished for me, so clear and definite must faith be in the work that the Holy Spirit accomplishes in me, to work in me the willing and the performing of all that is necessary for my salvation.

CHAPTER 23

The Leading of the Spirit

"As many as are led by the Spirit of God, they are the sons of God. The Spirit [himself] beareth witness with our spirit, that we are the children of God" (Rom. 8:14, 16).

It is the very same Spirit who leads us as children who also assures us that we are children. Without His leading there can be no assurance of our relationship. Full assurance of faith is enjoyed by him who surrenders himself entirely to the leading of the Spirit.

In what does this leading consist? Chiefly in this, that our whole inner life is guided by Him to what it ought to be. This we must firmly believe. Our growth and increase, our development and progress, is not our work but His; we are to trust Him for this. As a tree or animal grows and becomes large by the life which God has given to it, so also does the Christian grow by the Spirit of life in Christ Jesus.[1] We should be delighted with the assurance that the Spirit whom the Father gives to us will with divine wisdom and power guide our hidden life and bring it where God will have it.

Then there are also special directions of this leading. "He will lead you into all the truth." When we read the Word of God, we are to wait upon Him to make us experience the truth, the essential power of what God says. He makes the Word living and powerful. He leads us into a life corresponding to the Word.[2]

---

[1]Hos. 14:6, 7; Matt. 6:28; Mark 4:26, 28; Luke 2:40; Rom. 8:2
[2]John 6:63; 14:26; 16:13; 1 Cor. 2:10, 14; 1 Thess. 2:13

When you pray, you can count upon His leading: "The Spirit helpeth our infirmities." He leads us to what we must desire. He leads us into the way in which we are to pray—trustfully, persistently, mightily.[3]

In the way of sanctification it is He who will lead. He leads us in the path of righteousness. He leads us into all the will of God.[4]

In our speaking and working for the Lord, He will lead. Every child has the Spirit; every child has need of Him to know and to do the work of the Father. Without Him no child can please or serve the Father. The leading of the Spirit is the blessed privilege and the only power of a child of God.[5]

And how, then, can you fully enjoy this leading? The first thing that is necessary for this is *faith*. You must take time, new believer, to have your heart filled with the deep and living consciousness that the Spirit is in you. Read all the glorious declarations of your Father in His Word concerning what the Spirit is in you and for you until the conviction wholly fills you that you are a temple of the Spirit. Ignorance or unbelief on this point makes it impossible for the Spirit to speak in you and to lead you. Maintain the assurance that the Spirit of God dwells in you.[6]

The second thing that is necessary is this: you are to *hold yourself still*, to attend to the voice of the Spirit. As the Lord Jesus acts, so also does the Spirit: "He shall not cry, nor lift up his voice." He whispers gently and quietly; only the soul that sets itself very silently toward God can perceive His voice and guidance.

When we become, to a needless extent, engrossed in the world—with its business, its cares, its enjoyments, its literature, its politics—the Spirit cannot lead us. When our service to God is a bustling and working in our own wisdom and strength, the Spirit cannot be heard in us. It is the weak, the

---

[3]Zech. 12:10; Rom. 8:26, 27; Jude 20
[4]1 Thess. 5:23, 24; 1 Pet. 1:2, 15
[5]Matt. 10:20; Acts 1:8; Rom. 8:9, 13; Gal. 4:6; Eph. 1:13
[6]Acts 19:2; Rom. 5:5; 1 Cor. 3:16; 2 Cor. 5:5; Gal. 3:5, 14

simple, who are willing to be taught in humility, who receive the leading of the Spirit. Sit down every morning, sit down often in the day, to say, "Lord Jesus, I know nothing. I will be silent. Let the Spirit lead me."[7]

Third: *be obedient.* Listen to the inner voice and do what it says to you. Fill your heart every day with the Word, and when the Spirit puts you in mind of what the Word says, do it. Then you become capable of further teaching. It is to the obedient that the full blessing of the Spirit is promised.[8]

New believer, know that you are a temple of the Spirit and that it is only through the daily leading of the Spirit that you can walk as a child of God with the witness that you are pleasing the Father.

Precious Savior, imprint this lesson deeply on my mind. The Holy Spirit is in me. His leading is every day and everywhere indispensable for me. I cannot hear His voice in the Word when I do not wait silently upon Him. Lord, let a holy cautiousness keep watch over me that I may always walk as a student of the Spirit. Amen.

1. It is often asked: How do I know that I shall continue standing, that I shall be kept, that I shall grow? The question dishonors the Holy Spirit; it shows that you do not know Him or do not trust Him. The question indicates that you are seeking the secret of strength for perseverance in yourself and not in the Holy Spirit, your heavenly Guide.

2. As God sees that every moment there is air for me to breathe, so shall the Holy Spirit unceasingly maintain life in the hidden depths of my soul. He will not break off His own work.

3. From the time that we receive the Holy Spirit, we have nothing to do but to honor His work, to keep our hands off from it, to trust Him, and to let Him work.

4. The beginning and the end of the work of the Spirit is

---

[7]1 Chron. 19:12; Ps. 62:2; 131:2; Isa. 42:2; Hab. 2:20; Zech. 4:6; Acts 1:4
[8]John 14:15, 16; Acts 5:32

to reveal Jesus to me and to cause me to abide in Him. As soon as I try to control the work of the Spirit in me, I hinder Him. He cannot work when I am not willing to look upon Jesus.

5. The voice of the Father, the voice of the Good Shepherd, the voice of the Holy Spirit is very gentle. We must learn to become deaf to other voices, to the world and its news of friends and their thoughts, to our own ego and its desires; then shall we distinguish the voice of the Spirit. Let us often sit silently in prayer, entirely silent, to offer up our will and our thoughts, and with our eye upon Jesus to keep ear and heart open for the voice of the Spirit.

CHAPTER 24

Grieving the Spirit

"Grieve not the Holy Spirit of God, whereby ye are sealed unto the day of redemption" (Eph. 4:30).

It is by the Holy Spirit that the child of God is sealed—separated and stamped and marked as the possession of God. This sealing is not a dead or external action that is finished once for all. *It is a living process* which has power in the soul and gives firm assurance of faith only when it is experienced through the life of the Spirit in us. On this account we are to take great care not to grieve the Spirit; in Him alone can you daily have the joyful certainty and the full blessing of your sonship.

It is the same Spirit who leads us who witnesses with our spirit that we are children of God. And how can anyone grieve the Spirit? Above all, by yielding to sin. He is the Holy Spirit, given to sanctify us and, for every sin from which the blood cleanses us, to fill us with the holy life of God—with God. Sin grieves Him.[1] For this reason the Word of God presently states by name the sins against which above all we are to be on our guard. Mark only the four great sins that Paul mentions in connection with our text.

There is first *lying*. There is no single sin that in the Bible is so brought into connection with the devil as lying. Lying is from hell, and it goes on to hell. God is the God of truth. And the Holy Spirit cannot possibly carry forward His blessed working in a man or woman that lies, that is insincere, that

---

[1]Isa. 53:10; Acts 7:51; Heb. 10:29

does injury to the truth. New believer, review with care what the Word of God says about lying and liars, take care that you may never speak anything but the literal truth. Grieve not the Holy Spirit of God.[2]

Then there is *anger*. "Let all bitterness, and wrath, and anger, and clamor, and evil-speaking, be put away from you." Hastiness, proneness to anger, sin of temper is, along with lying, the most common sin by which the believer is kept back from increase in grace.[3] Believer, let all passionateness be put away from you; this follows on the command not to grieve the Spirit. Believe that the Holy Spirit, the great power of God, is in you. Surrender yourself every day to His indwelling in faith that Jesus can keep you by Him. He will make and keep you gentle. I believe in the power of God and of Jesus and of the Holy Spirit to overcome temper.[4] Confess the sin and God will cleanse you from it. Grieve not the Holy Spirit of God.

Then there is *stealing*: all sin against the property or possession of my neighbor; all deception and dishonesty in trade, whereby I do wrong to my neighbor and seek my own advantage at his cost. The law of Christ is love whereby I seek the advantage of my neighbor as well as my own. The love of money and property, which is inseparable from self-seeking, is incompatible with the leading of the Holy Spirit. The believer must be a man who is known as honest, righteous, and loving his neighbor as himself.[5]

Then says the apostle: "*no corrupt speech*, but such as is good for edifying as the case may be." Even the tongue of God's child belongs to his Lord. He must be known by his mode of speech. By his speaking he can grieve or please the Spirit. The sanctified tongue is a blessing not only to his neighbors but to the speaker himself. Foul talk, idle words,

[2]Ps. 5:6; Prov. 12:22; 21:28; John 8:44; Rev. 21:8, 27; 22:15

[3]Matt. 5:22; 1 Cor. 1:10, 11; 3:3; 13:1, 3; Gal. 5:5, 15, 21, 26; Col. 3:8, 12; 1 Thess. 5:15; James 3:14

[4]Matt. 11:29; 1 Cor. 6:19, 20; Gal. 6:1; Eph. 2:16, 17; Col. 1:8; 2 Tim. 1:12

[5]Luke 6:31; Rom. 13:10; 1 Thess. 4:6

foolish joking grieve the Holy Spirit. They make it impossible for the Spirit to sanctify and to comfort and to fill the heart with the love of God.[6]

New believer, I earnestly pray that you grieve not the Holy Spirit of God by these or other sins. If you have committed such sins, confess them and God will cleanse you from them. By the Holy Spirit you are sealed. If you would walk in the stability and joy of faith, listen to the word: "Grieve not the Holy Spirit of God."

Lord God, my Father in heaven, I pray that you would cause me to understand the marvelous grace you are manifesting to me, in that you have given me your Holy Spirit in my heart. Lord, let this faith be the argument and the power for cleansing me from every sin. Holy Jesus, sanctify me that in my thinking, speaking, acting—in all things—your image may appear. Amen.

1. The Christian's attitude toward this word, "grieve not the Holy Spirit," is a touchstone as to whether he understands the life of faith.

For some it is a word of terror and fear. A father once brought a child to the train to go on a journey with the new governess, with whom she was to remain. Before her departure he said, "I hear that she is very sensitive and misunderstands quickly. Take care that you do nothing to grieve her." The poor child had an unpleasant journey; she was living in the anxious fear of being misunderstood so easily.

This is the view of the Holy Spirit which many have: a Being who is difficult to satisfy, who thinks little of our weakness, and who, even though we take pain, is discontented when our work is not perfect.

2. Another father also brought his daughter to the train to go on a journey and to be a time away from home; but she was in company with her mother whom she loved very dearly.

---

[6]Prov. 10:19, 20, 21, 31; 18:20; Eccles. 5:1, 2; Matt. 12:36; Eph. 5:4; James 3:9, 10

"You are to be a good child," said the father, "and do everything to please your mother; otherwise you shall grieve her and me."

"Oh, certainly, Papa!" was the joyful answer of the child. For she felt so happy to be with her mother and was willing to do her utmost to be agreeable to her.

There are children of God to whom the Holy Spirit is so well known in His tender, helpful love and as the Comforter and the Good Spirit, that the word "grieve not the Spirit of God" has for them a gentle, encouraging power. May our fear to grieve Him always be the tender childlike fear of trustful love.

CHAPTER 25

Flesh and Spirit

"And I, brethren, could not speak unto you as unto spiritual, but as unto carnal, as unto babes in Christ" (1 Cor. 3:1).

"I am carnal, sold under sin. . . . To will is present with me; but how to perform that which is good I find not. . . . The law of the Spirit of life in Christ Jesus hath made me free from the law of sin and death. . . . Ye are not in the flesh, but in the Spirit, if so be that the Spirit of God dwell in you" (Rom. 7:14, 18; 8:2, 9).

"Having begun in the Spirit, are ye now made perfect by the flesh? . . . If ye be led of the Spirit, ye are not under the law. . . . If we live in the Spirit, let us also walk in the Spirit" (Gal. 3:3; 5:18, 25).

It is of great importance for the new believer to understand the difference between the flesh and the Spirit.

As long as strife and envy are still in the Christian, the Word of God calls him carnal. He would do good but he cannot; he does what he does not want to do, because he still strives in his own strength and not in the power of the Spirit.[1]

The flesh remains under the law and seeks to obey the law. But through the flesh the law is powerless and the endeavor to do good is vain. Its language is: "I am carnal, sold under sin: to will is present with me, but to do that which is good is not."[2]

This is not the condition in which God would have the

---

[1]Rom. 7:18; 1 Cor. 3:3; Gal. 5:15, 26
[2]Rom. 4:14, 15; 7:4, 6; 8:3, 8; Gal. 5:18; 6:12, 13; Heb. 7:18; 8:9, 13

believer remain. The Word says: "It is God that worketh in you, both to will and to work." The Christian must not only live in the Spirit but also walk in the Spirit. He must be a spiritual man and abide entirely under the leading of the Spirit.[3] He will no longer do what he would not. He will no longer remain in the condition of Romans 7—as a newborn babe, still seeking to fulfill the law—but he will now live in Romans 8, as one who through the Spirit is made free from the law with its commandment "Do this," which gives no power but brings death. He does not walk in the oldness of the letter but in the newness of the Spirit.[4]

There are Christians who begin with the Spirit but end with the flesh. They are converted, born again through the Spirit, but fall unconsciously into a life in which they endeavor to overcome sin and be holy through their own effort, through doing their best. They ask God to help them in these their endeavors and think that this is faith. They do not understand what it is to say, "In me, that is, in my flesh, dwelleth no good thing," and that they are to cease from their own endeavors in order to do God's will wholly and only through the Spirit.[5]

New believer, learn what it is to say of yourself, just as you are, even after the new birth: "I am carnal, sold under sin." *Endeavor no longer to be doing your best, and to be praying to God, and to be trusting Him to help you.* No, learn to say, "The law of the Spirit of life in Christ Jesus made me free from the law of sin and of death." Let your work every day be to have the Spirit work in you, to walk by the Spirit, and you shall be redeemed from the life of complaining, "The good that I would I do not," into a life of faith in which it is God who works in you both to will and to do.

Lord God, teach me to acknowledge with all my heart that in me—that is, in my flesh—dwelleth nothing good. Teach me

---

[3]Rom. 8:14; 1 Cor. 2:15; 3:1; Gal. 6:1
[4]Rom. 7:6; 8:2, 13
[5]Rom. 7:18; Gal. 3:3; 4:9; 5:4, 7

*to cease from every thought as if I could with my own en-
deavors serve or please you. Teach me to understand that the
Spirit is the Comforter, who frees me from all anxiety and fear
about my own powerlessness in order that He may work the
strength of Christ in me. Amen.*

1. In order to understand the conflict between flesh and
Spirit, we must especially seek to have clear insight into the
connection between Romans 7 and 8. In Rom. 7:6 Paul had
spoken of the twofold way of serving God: the one in the
oldness of the letter, the other in the newness of the Spirit.
In Rom. 7:14–16 he describes the first; in Rom. 8:1–16, the
second. This appears clearly when we observe that in chapter
7 he mentions the Spirit only once, the law more than twenty
times; in chapter 8, verses 1–16, he speaks of the Spirit six-
teen times. In Romans 7 we see the regenerate soul just as
he is in the flesh, desirous but powerless to fulfill the law,
mourning as one who is "captive under the law of sin." In
Romans 8 we hear him say, "The law of the Spirit of life in
Christ Jesus hath made me free from the law of sin." Romans
7 describes the condition of the Christian, contemplated as
renewed but not experiencing by faith the power of the Holy
Spirit; Romans 8 describes his life in the freedom which the
Spirit of God really gives from the power of sin.

2. In order to clarify the difference between the two
methods of serving God, let me list passages in which they
are expressed with special distinctness. Compare them with
care. Ask that the Spirit will help you understand them.
Study the following scripture passages and take deeply to
heart the lesson as to how you are to serve God well and how
not.

The circumcision of the heart, in the Spirit, not in the
letter (Rom. 2:29).

To him that works not but believes, his faith is reckoned
for righteousness (Rom. 4:5).

You are not under the law but under grace (Rom. 6:14).

We have been discharged from the law, so that we serve

in newness of the Spirit and not in the oldness of the letter (Rom. 7:6).

We know that the law is spiritual, but I am carnal, sold under sin (Rom. 8:4).

Ye received not the Spirit of bondage again to fear but ye received the Spirit of adoption (Rom. 8:15).

The righteousness which is of the law is: "The man that doeth these things shall live by them. But the righteousness which is of faith saith thus, Say not in thine heart, Who shall ascend? Who shall descend? But what saith it? The word is nigh thee, in thy mouth, and in thy heart" (Rom. 10:5–8).

If it is by grace, it is no more of works (Rom. 11:6).

I could not speak unto you as unto spiritual, but as unto carnal, as unto babes in Christ (1 Cor. 3:1).

I live; and yet no longer I, but Christ liveth in me (Gal. 2:20).

The righteous shall live by faith; yet the law is not of faith: but the man that doeth these things shall live by them (Gal. 3:11, 12).

If the inheritance is of the law, it is no more of promise (Gal. 3:18).

So that thou art no longer a bondservant, but a son (Gal. 4:7).

Wherefore, brethren, we are not children of a handmaid, but of the free-woman (Gal. 4:31).

Walk by the Spirit and you shall not fulfill the lust of the flesh (Gal. 5:16).

If you are led by the Spirit, you are not under the law (Gal. 5:18).

Who worship by the Spirit of God and glory in Christ Jesus, and have no confidence in the flesh (Phil. 3:8).

Another priest, who hath been made not after the law of a carnal commandment, but after the power of an endless life (Heb. 8:16).

3. Beloved believer, you have received the Holy Spirit from the Lord Jesus to reveal Him and His life in you and to mortify the working of the body of sin. Earnestly pray to be filled with the Spirit. Live in the joyful faith that the

Spirit is in you, as your Comforter and Teacher, and that through Him all will be accomplished. Learn by heart this verse and let it live in your heart and on your lips: "We are the circumcision, who worship by the Spirit of God and glory in Christ Jesus, and have no confidence in the flesh."

CHAPTER 26

The Life of Faith

"The just shall live by his faith" (Hab. 2:4).

"We are delivered from the law . . . that we should serve in newness of spirit, and not in the oldness of the letter" (Rom. 7:6).

"I live; yet not I, but Christ liveth in me: and the life which I now live in the flesh I live by the faith of the Son of God, who loved me, and gave himself for me" (Gal. 2:20).

The word from Habakkuk is quoted three times in the New Testament as the divine representation of salvation in Christ by faith alone.[1] But the word is oftentimes misunderstood, as if it meant: "Man shall on his conversion be justified by faith." The word includes this but signifies much more. It says that the righteous shall *live* by faith; the whole life of the righteous, from moment to moment, shall be by faith.[2]

We know the sharp distinction which God in His Word presents between the grace that comes by faith and the law that demands works. This is generally admitted with reference to justification. But that distinction holds just as much for the whole life of sanctification. The righteous shall live by faith alone—that is, shall have power to live according to the will of God. As at his conversion he found it necessary to understand that there was nothing good in him and that he must receive grace as one that was powerless and godless,

---

[1]Rom. 1:17; Gal. 3:11; Heb. 10:38
[2]Rom. 5:17, 21; 6:11; 8:2; Gal. 2:20; 1 John 5:11, 12

103

so as a believer he must receive his power for good every moment from above.[3]

His work, therefore, must be every morning and every hour to look up and believe and receive his power from above, out of his Lord in heaven. *I am not to do what I can, and hope in the Lord to supply strength.* No, as one who has been dead, who is literally able for nothing in himself and whose life is in his Lord above, I am to depend wholly on Him who will work in me mightily.[4]

Happy is the believer who understands that his greatest danger is to fall under the law and to endeavor to serve God in the flesh with his own strength—happy when he discerns that he is not under the law which only demands and yet is powerless through the flesh, but is under grace where he simply has to receive what has been given; happy when he fully appropriates for himself the promise of the Spirit who transfers all that is in Christ to himself; happy when he understands what it is to live by faith and to serve not in the oldness of the letter but in the newness of the Spirit.[5]

Let us make the words of Paul our own, for they present to us the true life of faith: "I have been crucified with Christ; yet I live." My flesh—not only my sin, but my flesh—*all that is of myself, my own living and willing, my own power and working*—have I given up to death. I live no longer; of myself, I cannot. I will not live or do anything.[6] Christ lives in me: He, by His Spirit, is my power and teaches and strengthens me to live as I ought to do. And that life which I now live in the flesh, I live by faith in Him. My great work is to depend upon Him to work in me the willing as well as the accomplishment.

New believer, let this life of faith be your faith.

O my Lord Jesus, you are my life—yes, my life. You live

---

[3]Rom. 7:18; 8:2, 13; Heb. 11:33

[4]Rom. 4:17; 2 Cor. 1:9; Col. 1:29; 2:3

[5]Rom. 7:4, 6; 12:5, 6; Gal. 5:18; Phil. 3:3

[6]John 15:4, 5; 1 Cor. 15:10; 2 Cor. 12:9, 10

in me and are willing to take my whole life under your own supervision. My whole life may daily be a joyful trust and experience that you are working all in me.

Precious Lord, to that life of faith will I surrender myself. Yes, to you I surrender myself to teach me and to reveal yourself fully in me. Amen.

1. Do you discern the error of the expression, "If the Lord helps me"; "the Lord must help me"? In natural things we speak like this, for we have a certain measure of power, and the Lord will increase it. But the New Testament never uses the expression "help" for the grace of God in the soul. We have absolutely no power; God is not to help us because we are weak. No, He is to give His life and His power in us as those who are entirely powerless. He that discerns this will learn to live by faith alone.

2. "Without faith it is impossible to please God." "All that is not of faith is sin." Such words of the Spirit of God teach us how every deed and disposition of our life is to be full of faith.

3. Our first work every day is to afresh exercise faith in Jesus as our life, to believe that He dwells in us and will do all for us and in us. This faith must be the mood of our soul the whole day. This faith cannot be maintained except in the fellowship and nearness of Jesus himself.

4. This faith has its power in the mutual surrender of Jesus and the believer to each other. Jesus first gives himself wholly for us. The believer gives himself wholly in order to be taken into possession and guided by Jesus. Then the soul cannot begin to doubt if He will do all for it.

CHAPTER 27

The Might of Satan

"Simon, Simon, behold, Satan hath desired to have you, that he may sift you as wheat: but I have prayed for thee, that thy faith fail not" (Luke 22:31, 32).

There is nothing that makes an enemy so dangerous as the fact that he remains hidden or forgotten. Of the three great enemies of the Christian—the world, the flesh, and the devil—the last is the most dangerous, not only because it is he who, strictly speaking, lends to the others what power they have, but also because he is not seen and, therefore, little known or feared. The devil has the power of darkness; he darkens the eyes so that men do not know him. He surrounds himself with darkness so that he is not observed. He has even the power to appear as an angel of light.[1] It is by the faith that recognizes unseen things that the believer is to endeavor to know Satan even as the Scripture has revealed him.

When the Lord Jesus was living upon earth, His great work was to overcome Satan. When at His baptism He was filled with the Spirit, this fullness of the Spirit brought him into contact with Satan as the head of the world of evil spirits, to combat him and to overcome him.[2] After that time the eyes of the Lord were always perceptive to the power and working of Satan. In all sin and misery He was the revelation of the mighty kingdom of the very same superior, the evil

---

[1]Matt. 4:6; 2 Cor. 4:4; 11:14
[2]Matt. 4:1, 10

one. Not only in the demoniacs but also in the sick, He saw the enemy of God and man.[3] In the advice of Peter to avoid the cross and in his denial of the Lord, where we would think it simply the revelation of the natural character of Peter, Jesus saw the work of Satan.[4] In His own suffering, where we would speak of the sin of man and the permission of God, Jesus perceived the power of darkness. His whole work in living and dying was to destroy the works of Satan, and He shall also at His second coming utterly destroy Satan.[5]

His word to Peter, compared with the personal experience of the Lord, gives us a fearful insight into the work of the enemy. "Satan hath eagerly desired you," says Jesus. "As a roaring lion, he walketh about, seeking whom he may devour," says Peter himself later on.[6] He does not have unlimited power, but he is always eager to make use of every weak or unguarded moment.

"That he might sift you as wheat": what a picture! This world, yes, even the Church of Christ, is the threshing floor of Satan. The corn belongs to God; the chaff is Satan's. He sifts and sifts continually, and all that falls through with the chaff he endeavors to take for himself. There are many believers who fall through in a terrible fashion, and who, were it not for the intercession of their Lord, would perish forever.[7]

Satan has more than one sieve. The first is generally *worldly-mindedness*—the love of the world. Many are pious in their time of poverty; but when they become rich, they eagerly strive to win the world. Or in the times of conversion and awakening, they appear very zealous, but through the care of the world they are led astray.[8]

A second sieve is *self-love* and *self-seeking*. Whenever anyone does not give himself undividedly to serve his Lord

[3]Matt. 12:28; Mark 4:15; Luke 13:16; Acts 10:38
[4]Matt. 16:23; Luke 22:31, 32
[5]Luke 10:18; 22:3, 53; John 12:31; 14:30; 16:11; Rom. 16:20; Col. 2:15; 2 Thess. 2:8, 9; 1 John 3:8
[6]1 Cor. 7:5; 2 Cor. 2:10, 11; 1 Pet. 5:8
[7]1 Cor. 5:5; 1 Tim. 1:20
[8]Matt. 4:9; 13:22; 1 Tim. 6:9, 10; 2 Tim. 4:10

and his neighbor and to love his neighbor in the Lord, it soon appears that the principal characteristic of a disciple is lacking in him. It will be manifest that many, with a fair profession of being devoted to the service of God, fail utterly at this point and must be counted with the chaff. Lovelessness is the sure characteristic of the power of Satan.[9]

Yet another sieve—a very dangerous one—is *self-confidence*. Under the name of following the Spirit, one may listen to the thoughts of his own heart. He is zealous for the Lord, but with a carnal zeal in which the gentleness of the Lamb of God is not seen. Without being observed, the movements of the flesh mingle with the workings of the Spirit; and while he boasts that he is overcoming Satan, he is actually being secretly ensnared by him.[10]

Oh, it is a serious life here upon earth, where God gives Satan permission to set his threshing floor even in the church. Happy are they who with deep humility, with fear and trembling, distrust themselves. Our only security is in the intercession and guidance of Him who overcame Satan.[11] May the idea that we know all the depths of Satan and are a match for all his cunning strategies be far from us. It is in the region of the spirit, in the invisible as well as in the visible, that he works and has power. Let us fear lest, while we have known and overcome him in the visible, he should prevail over us in the spiritual. May our only security be the conviction of our frailty and weakness combined with our confidence in Him who certainly keeps the lowly in heart.

Lord Jesus, open our eyes to know our enemy and his deceptions. Cause us to see him and his realm that we may dread all that is of him. And open our eyes to see how you have overcome him and how in you we are invincible. Oh, teach us what it is to be in you, to mortify all that is simply of ourselves and the will of the flesh, and to be strong in weakness and

---

[9]John 8:44; 1 John 3:10, 15; 4:20
[10]Gal. 3:3; 5:13
[11]Eph. 6:10, 12, 16

lowliness. And teach us to bring into prayer the conflict of faith against every stronghold of Satan, because we know that you will bruise him under our feet. Amen.

1. What comfort does the knowledge of the existence of Satan give us? We know, then, that sin is derived from a foreign power which has thrust itself into our nature, and does not naturally belong to us. We also know that he has been entirely defeated by the Lord Jesus, and thus has no power over us as long as we abide trustfully in Christ.

2. The whole of this world, with all that is in it, is under the domination of Satan; therefore, there is nothing, even what appears good and fair, that may not be dangerous for us. In all things, even in what is lawful and right, we must be led and sanctified by the Spirit if we would continue liberated from the power of Satan.

3. Satan is an evil spirit; only by the good Spirit, the Spirit of God, can we offer resistance to him. He works in the invisible. In order to combat him, we must, by prayer, enter into the invisible. He is a mighty prince; only in the name of One who is mightier and in fellowship with Him can we overcome.

4. What a glorious work is the labor for the lost—a conflict to rescue them from the power of Satan (Acts 26:18).

5. In Revelation, the victory over Satan is ascribed to the blood of the Lamb (Rev. 12:11). Believers have also testified that there is no power in temptation, because Satan readily retreats when one appeals to the blood, by which one knows that sin has been entirely expiated and we are thus also wholly freed from his power.

CHAPTER 28

The Conflict of the Christian

"Strive to enter in at the straight gate" (Luke 13:24).
"Fight the good fight of faith" (1 Tim. 6:12).
"I have fought a good fight, I have finished my course, I have kept the faith" (2 Tim. 4:7).

These verses speak of a twofold conflict. The first is addressed to the unconverted: "Strive to enter in by the narrow door." Entrance by a door is the work of a moment; the sinner is not to strive to enter during his whole lifetime; he is to strive and do it immediately. He is not to allow anything to hold him back; he must enter in.[1]

Then comes the second, the lifelong conflict: by the narrow door I come upon the new way. On the new way there are still many enemies. Of this lifelong conflict Paul says: "I have fought a good fight, I have finished my course, I have kept the faith." With respect to the continuous conflict, he gives the charge, "Fight the good fight of faith."

There is much misunderstanding about this twofold conflict. Many strive all their life against the Lord and His callings, and because they are not at rest but feel an inner conflict, they think that this is the conflict of a believer. They are deceived. This is the struggle of a person who is not willing to abandon everything and surrender himself to the Lord.[2] This is not the conflict that the Lord leads us into. He says that the conflict concerned with entering is not a conflict lasting years. No, He desires that you should break through

---

[1]Gen. 19:22; John 10:9; 2 Cor. 6:2; Heb. 4:6, 7
[2]Acts 5:39; 1 Cor. 10:22

111

the enemies that would hold you back, and immediately enter in.

Then follows the second conflict, which endures for life. Paul twice calls this the fight of faith. The chief characteristic of it is faith. He who understands that the principle element in the battle is to believe, and acts accordingly, will be victorious—just as in another passage Paul says to the believer: "Withal taking up the shield of faith, wherewith ye shall be able to quench all the fiery darts of the evil one."[3]

And what, then, does it mean, this "fight of faith"? That while I strive I am to believe that the Lord will help me? No, it is not that, although it is often understood as such.

In a conflict it is of supreme importance that I be in a stronghold or fortress which cannot be taken. With such a stronghold a weak garrison can offer resistance to a powerful enemy. Our conflict as believers is now no longer concerned with going into the fortress. No, we have gone in and are now in; and so long as we remain in it, we are invincible. The stronghold is Christ.[4] By faith we are in Him; by faith we know that the enemy can make no progress against our fortress.

The wiles of Satan all go forth in the direction of enticing us out of our fortress, of engaging us in conflict with him on the open plain. There he always overcomes. But if we only strive in faith, we overcome because Satan then has to deal with Him and because He then fights and overcomes.[5] "This is the victory that hath overcome the world, even our faith."

The reason the victory is only by faith and the fight of faith is the good fight is this: it is the Lord Jesus who purchased the victory and who alone gives power and dominion over the enemy. If we are, and abide, in Him and surrender ourselves to live in Him and by faith appropriate what He is, then the victory is in itself our own. We then understand, "The battle is not yours, but God's. The Lord your God shall

---

[3]Eph. 6:16; 1 John 5:4, 5
[4]Ps. 18:2, 3; 46:1, 2; 62:2, 3, 6–8; 144:2; Eph. 6:10
[5]Ex. 14:14; Josh. 5:14; John 16:33; Rom. 8:37; 2 Cor. 2:14

112

fight for you, and ye shall be still." Just as we in opposition
to God can achieve nothing good of ourselves, but in Christ
please Him, so it is in opposition to Satan: in ourselves we
achieve nothing, but in Christ we are more than conquerors.
By faith we stand in Him righteous before God, and in Him
we are strong against our enemies.[6]

In this light we can read and take home for ourselves all
the noble passages in the Old Testament, especially in the
Psalms, where the glorious conflict of God in behalf of His
people is spoken of. Fear, or spiritlessness, or uncertainty,
makes weak and cannot overcome; faith in the living God is
equal to everything.[7] In Christ this truth is now still more
real. God has come near. His power works in us who believe;
it is really He who fights for us.

*O Lord Jesus, the Prince of the army of the Lord, the Hero,
the Victor, teach me to be strong in you, my stronghold, and
in the power of your might. Teach me to understand what the
good fight of faith is and how the one thing that I have need
of is always to look to you—to you, the supreme guide of faith.
And consequently in me, too, let this be the victory that over-
cometh the world—namely, my faith. Amen.*

1. The conflict of faith is not a civil war in which one half
of the kingdom is divided against the other. This would be
insurrection. This is the one conflict that many Christians
know: the unrest of the conscience and the powerless wres-
tling of a will which consents to that which is good but does
not perform it. The Christian has not to overcome himself.
This his Lord does when he surrenders himself. Then he is
free and strong to combat and overcome the enemies of his
Lord and of the kingdom. No sooner, however, are we willing
that God should have His way in us than we are found striving against God. This also is truly conflict, but it is not the
good fight of faith.

[6]Ps. 44:4–8; Isa. 45:24
[7]Deut. 20:3, 8; Josh. 6:20; Judg. 7:3; Ps. 18:32–40; Heb. 11:23

2. In Galatians 5, reference is made to this inner conflict; for the Galatians had not yet entirely surrendered themselves to the Spirit to walk after the Spirit. "The connection," says Lange, "shows that this conflict between the flesh and the Spirit of God is not endless, but that there is expected of the Christian a complete surrender of himself in order to be led only by the one principle—the Spirit—and then, further, a refusal to obey the flesh." The believer must not strive against the flesh to overcome it; this he cannot do. What he is to do is to choose to whom he will subject himself. By the surrender of faith to Christ to strive in Him through the Spirit, he has a divine power for overcoming.

3. Hence, as we have seen in connection with the beginning of the new life, our one work every day and the whole day is to believe. Out of faith come all blessings and powers, and also the victory for overcoming.

CHAPTER 29

Be a Blessing

"Get thee out of thy country, and from thy kindred, and from thy father's house, unto a land that I will show thee; and I will make of thee a great nation, and I will bless thee; and thou shalt be a blessing" (Gen. 12:1, 2).

In these first words that God spoke to Abraham, we have the short summary of all that God has to say to him and to us as His children. We see the goal to which God calls us, the power that carries us to that goal, and the place where the power is found.

Be a blessing: that is the goal for which God separates Abraham and every believer.

God would have us understand that when He blesses us, this is not simply to make us happy but that we should still further communicate His blessing.[1] God is love, and therefore He blesses. Love seeks not itself; when the love of God comes to us, it will seek others through us.[2] The new believer must understand that he has received grace with the definite goal of becoming a blessing to others. Keep not for yourself what the Lord gives to you for others. Offer yourself expressly and completely to the Lord to be used by Him for others; that is the way to overflowing blessing.[3]

The power for this work will be given. "Be a blessing," "I

---

[1]Matt. 5:44, 45; 10:8; 18:33

[2]Isa. 58:10, 11; 1 Cor. 13:5; 1 John 4:11

[3]Ps. 112: 5, 9; Prov. 11:24, 25; Matt. 25:40; 1 Cor. 15:58; 2 Cor. 9:6; Heb. 6:10

will bless thee," says the Lord. You are to be personally sanctified and filled with the Spirit and peace and power of the Lord; then you have power to bless.[4] In Christ God has "blessed us with all spiritual things." Let Jesus fill you with these blessings and you shall certainly be a blessing. You need not doubt or fear.

The blessing of God includes in it the power of life for multiplication, for expansion, for communication. See in the Scriptures how blessing and multiplication go together.[5] Blessing always includes the power to bless others. Only give the word of the Almighty God "I will bless thee" time to sink into your spirit. Wait upon God that He may say to you, "I will bless thee." Let your faith hold to this. God will make it truth to you above all asking and thinking.[6]

But to arrive at the goal you must also commit yourself to the place of blessing, the land of promise, the simple life of faith in the promises. "Get thee out of thy land and thy father's house," says the Lord. Departure, separation from the life of sin and the flesh is what God would have. The offering up of what is most precious to man is the way to the blessing of God.[7] "Get thee to a land that I will show thee," says the Lord—out of the old life to a new life, where I alone am your guide; that is, a life where God can have me wholly for himself, where I walk only on the promises of God—a life of faith.

Believer, God will fulfill in you His promise, "I will bless thee." Oh, go out of your land and your father's house, out of the life of sin and the flesh, out of fellowship with the flesh and this world, to the new life—the life of the Spirit, the life in fellowship with God to which He will lead you. There you become receptive to His blessing; there your heart becomes open to full faith in His word, "I will bless thee"; there He can fulfill that word to you and make you full of blessing and

---

[4]Luke 24:49; John 7:38; 14:12
[5]Gen. 1:22, 28; 9:1; 22:17; 26:24
[6]2 Cor. 9:8, 11; Eph. 1:3; Heb. 6:14
[7]Luke 18:29, 30; John 12:24, 25; 2 Cor. 6:17, 18

power to be a blessing to others. Live with God, separated from the world; then you shall hear the voice of God speak with power: "I will bless thee," "Be thou a blessing."

O my Father, show me the way to that promised land where you bring your people to have them wholly for yourself. I will abandon everything to follow you, to hold conversation with you alone, in order that you may fill me with your blessing. Lord, let your word "I will bless thee" live in my heart as the word of God; then I shall give myself wholly to live for others and to be a blessing. Amen.

1. God is the great, the only fountain of blessing; as much of God as I have in me, so much blessing can I bring. I can work for others without blessing. Actually to be a blessing, I must begin with that word, "I will bless thee"; then the other, "Be a blessing," becomes easy.

2. In order to become a blessing, begin on a small scale; surrender yourself up for others. Live to make others happy. Believe that the love of God dwells in you by the Spirit, and give yourself wholly to be a blessing and a joy to those who are round about you. Pray that God will shed abroad His love in you still further by the Spirit. And believe that God will make you a blessing to others.

3. This surrender must have time in solitary prayer that God may obtain possession of your spirit. This is for you the departure from your father's house—separate yourself from men so that God may speak with you.

4. What do you think? Was Abraham ever filled with regret that he placed himself so entirely under the leading of God? Then do likewise.

5. Do you now know the two words which are the source of all promises and all commands to the children of believing Abraham? The promise is: "I will bless thee." The command is: "Be a blessing." Take them both firmly for yourself.

6. Do you now understand where these two words to Abraham are fulfilled? In separation from his father's house—in the walk in fellowship with God.

CHAPTER 30

Personal Work

"Restore unto me the joy of thy salvation: and uphold me with thy free spirit. Then will I teach transgressors thy ways: and sinners shall be converted unto thee" (Ps. 51:12, 13).

"I believed, therefore have I spoken" (Ps. 116:10).

"But ye shall receive power, after that the Holy Spirit is come upon you" (Acts 1:8).

Every believer is called to be a witness for his Lord. Not only by a godly walk but by a personal effort must I serve and make known my Lord. My speech is one of the principal means of communication with others and influence upon them. It is but a half dedication when I do not also bring the offering of my lips to speak for the Lord.[1]

Of this work there is an inconceivably great need. There are thousands of believers who continually enjoy the preaching of the Word and yet do not understand the way of salvation. The Lord Jesus not only preached to the multitudes but also spoke to individuals according to their needs.[2] Scripture is full of examples of those who told others what the Lord had done for them, and who thus became a blessing to them.[3] The preacher alone cannot do this work of personal speaking; every believer must cooperate with him. He is in the world as a witness for his Lord. His own life cannot come

---

[1]Ps. 40:10, 11; 66:16; 71:8, 15, 24; Heb. 13:15
[2]Luke 7:40; John 3:3; 4:7
[3]Ex. 18:8, 11; 2 Chron. 5:13

to its fullness if he does not confess his Lord and work for Him.

That witness for the Lord must be a personal witness. We must have the courage to say, "He has redeemed me. He will also redeem you. Will you not accept this redemption? Come, let me show you the way."[4] There are hundreds who would be glad if the personal question were put to them: "Are you redeemed? What keeps you back? Can I help you to go to the Lord?" Parents ought to speak personally with their children and ask the question, "My child, have you already received the Lord Jesus?" Teachers in Sunday schools and in day schools when they teach the Word of God ought to bring forward the personal question, whether the children have really received salvation, and they ought to seek the opportunity of also putting the question to them separately. Friends must speak with their friends. Yes, before all else this work should be done.

Such work must be the work of love. People are to know that you love them tenderly. Let the humility and gentleness of love, as this was to be seen in Jesus, be seen also in you. At every turn surrender yourself to Jesus to be filled with His love; it is not by feeling but by faith in this love that you can do your work. "Beloved, keep yourselves in the love of God. And on some have mercy who are in doubt; and some save, snatching them out of the fire; and on some have mercy with fear." The flesh often thinks that strength and force do more than love and patience. But that is not so: love achieves everything; it has overcome on the cross.[5]

Such work must be the work of faith—faith working by love: faith that the Lord desires to use you and will use you. Be not afraid on account of your weakness; learn in the Scriptures what glorious promises God from time to time gave to those who had to speak for Him.[6] Surrender yourself continually to God to be used for the rescue of the lost. Take your

---

[4]John 1:41, 42, 46; 4:28, 29, 39; Acts 11:19

[5]Heb. 3:13; 10:24; Jude 21, 23

[6]Ex. 4:11, 12; Josh. 1:9; Isa. 50:4, 11; Jer. 1:6, 7; Matt. 10:19, 20

stand on the fact that He who has redeemed you for this purpose will for this purpose bless you.

Although your work is in weakness and fear, although no blessing appears to come, be of good courage; in His time we shall reap.[7] Be filled with faith in the power of God, in His blessing upon you, and in the certainty of the hearing of prayer. "If any man see his brother sinning a sin not unto death, he shall ask, and God will give him life." Whether it be the most miserable and neglected sinner or whether it be the decent but indiffernet sinner, take courage. The Lord is mighty to bless; He hears prayer.

Above all—for this is the principal point—carry out this work in fellowship with Jesus. Live close to Him; live entirely for Him; let Jesus be seen in all your life and He will speak and work in you.[8] Be full of the blessing of the Lord, full of His Spirit and His love, and it cannot be otherwise than that you should be a blessing. You will have the love and the courage, with all humility, to put to souls the question, "Is it well with you? Do you have the Lord Jesus as your Savior?" And the Lord will make you experience the rich blessing which is promised to those who live to bless others.

New believer, be a witness for Jesus. Live as one who is wholly surrendered to Him to watch and to work for His honor.

Blessed Lord Jesus, who has redeemed me to serve the Father in the proclamation of His love, I will with a willing spirit offer myself to you for this end. Fill my heart for this end with love to Him, to you, and to others. Cause me to see what an honor it is to do the work of redeeming love, even as you have done. Strengthen my confidence that you are working with your power in my weakness. And let my joy be to help souls to you. Amen.

1. The question is often asked, "What can I do to work

---

[7]2 Chron. 15:7; Ps. 126:6; Hag. 2:5; Gal. 6:9
[8]Acts 4:13; 2 Cor. 3:5; 13:3

for the Lord?" Could you take a class in the Sunday school? Perhaps you live in the country where there are children that have no Sunday school devoted to them. Perhaps there are children or adults in your area who do not go to church. See if you can gather them together in the name of Jesus. Make it a matter of prayer and faith. Although you do this work with trembling, you may be sure that to begin to work will make you strong.

Or can you do something with the circulation of books and literature? When you have a book that has been useful to you, order six or twelve copies of it. Speak of it, and offer it to others; you can do great service by this means. So also with tracts. You may obtain blessing by this method. It will especially help you to speak to others if you begin with telling what is in a book.

2. But the principal thing is personal speaking. Do not hold back because you feel no freedom. The Lord will give you freedom in His own time. It is incredible how many are lost through ignorance. No one has ever personally made it clear to them how they can be saved. Realize that people are full of erroneous ideas, people misunderstand everything. Begin then to speak and to help souls to understand that they are to receive Jesus just as they are, that they can certainly know that He receives them, and that this is the power of a new and holy life.

CHAPTER 31

Missionary Work

"And he said unto them, Go ye into all the world, and preach the gospel to every creature. And they went forth, and preached everywhere, the Lord working with them, and confirming the word with signs following" (Mark 16:15, 20).

Every friend of Jesus is a friend of missions. Where there is a healthy spiritual life, there is a love for the missionary cause. When you consider the reasons for this, you obtain an insight into the glory of missions and into your calling to embrace this cause as a part of your life. Come and hear how much there is to make missionary work glorious and precious.

1. *It is the cause for which Jesus left the throne of heaven.* The lost are His inheritance, given to Him by His Father. It is among the lost that the power of Satan has been established. Jesus must have himself vindicated as the conqueror. His glory, the coming and manifestation of His kingdom, depend on missions.[1]

2. *Missionary work is the principal aim of the church on earth.* All the last words of the Lord Jesus teach us this.[2] The Lord is the head and has made himself dependent upon His body, upon His members, by whom alone He can do His work.[3] As a member of Christ, as a member of the church, shall I not give myself to take part that this goal may be reached?

---

[1]Ps. 2:3; Matt. 24:14; 28:18, 19, 20; Mark 13:10; Luke 21:24; Rom. 11:25
[2]Mark 16:15; Luke 24:47; John 17:18; Acts 1:8
[3]1 Cor. 12:21

122

3. *It is the work for which the Holy Spirit was given.* See this in the promise of the Spirit; in the leading of the Spirit granted to Peter and Barnabas and Saul.[4] In the history of the Church we find that times of revival go hand in hand with new zeal for the missionary cause. The Holy Spirit is always a holy enthusiast for the extension of the kingdom.

4. *Missionary work brings blessing on the Church.* It rouses to heroic deeds of faith and self-denial. It has furnished the most glorious instances of the wondrous power of the Lord. It gives heavenly joy over the conversion of sinners to those who watch for it with love and prayer. It strengthens the heart to understand God's plans and to be involved in the fulfillment of them. Missionary work is a symbol of the life of God in a church and brings more life.[5]

5. *What a blessing it is for the world!* What would we have been had not missionaries come to our heathen forefathers in Europe? Has not missionary work already won a glorious victory in some lands? What help is there for the millions of lost, if not in missions?[6] Heaven and hell look upon missions as the battlefield where the powers of Satan and of Jesus Christ encounter one another. Alas! that the conflict should be carried on so feebly.

6. *There will be a blessing for your own soul in love for missionary work.*[7] You will be exercised in faith. Missionary work is a cause for faith, where patience must be exercised and the ways of men put away. You must learn to cleave to God and the Word.

Love will be awakened. You will learn to go out of yourselves and your little circle and with an open and a large heart to live in the interests of your Lord and King. You will feel how little love you have, but you will receive more love.

You will be drawn into prayer. Your calling and power as an intercessor will become clearer to you, and therewith

---

[4]Acts 1:8; 11:12, 23, 24; 13:2, 4; 22:21
[5]Acts 14:27; 15:4, 5; Rom. 11:25, 33; 15:10; Eph. 3:5, 8, 10
[6]Isa. 49:6, 12, 18, 22; 54:1, 2
[7]Prov. 11:24, 25; Isa. 58:7, 8

the blessedness of thus cooperating for the kingdom. You will discern that it is the highest conformity to Him who came to seek the lost, to give up your own ease and rest to fight in love the fight of prayer against Satan in behalf of the lost.

New believer, missionary work is more glorious and holy than you suppose. There is more blessing in it than you are aware of. The new life in you depends upon it more than you can as yet understand. Yield yourself in obedience to the Word to give missions a large place in your heart; yes, in your heart. The Lord himself will further teach and bless you.

And if you would increase your love for missions, as the work of your Lord, attend to the following hints: Become acquainted with the missionary cause. Endeavor through literature and books to know what the condition and needs of the world are; what, by the blessing of the Lord, has been done already; what the work is that is being done now.

Speak with others about this cause. Perhaps you could institute in your neighborhood a little missionary society.

Perhaps one of your prayer meetings—say, once a month, could be set apart for prayer in behalf of the missionary cause. Pray also for this in private. Let the coming of the kingdom have a definite place in your private prayers. Endeavor to follow the material concerning prayer for the lost in the promises of the Word, especially in the prophet Isaiah.[8]

Also give to missions; not only when you are asked, not merely what you can spare without feeling it. But set apart for this cause a portion of what you possess or earn.

Be earnest about the Lord's work. If there is mission work that is being done in your neighborhood, show yourself a friend to it. Although there may be imperfection in that work—and where is there work of man that is perfect?—do not complain of the imperfection but look upon the essence of the cause—the endeavor to obey the command of the Lord— and give your prayer and your help. A friend of Jesus is a

---

[8]Isa. 49:6, 18, 21, 22; 54:1, 3; 60:1, 3, 11, 16; 62:2

friend of missions. Love for missionary work is an indispensable element of the new life.

Son of God, when you breathed your Spirit upon the disciples, saying, "Receive ye the Holy Ghost," you added: "As the Father hath sent me, even so send I you." Lord, here am I. Send me also. Breathe your Spirit into me also that I may live for your kingdom. Amen.

1. "Unknown makes unbeloved" is a word that is true of missionary work. He who is acquainted with the wonders that God has wrought in some lands will praise and thank God for what the missionary enterprise has achieved, and will be strengthened in his faith that missionary work is really God's own cause.

Among books that help to awaken interest in missions are biographies of missionaries. Some books on missions are generally to be found in our church libraries.

2. We should never forget that the missionary cause is an enterprise of faith. It requires faith in the promises of God, in the power of God. It has need of love—love to Jesus, whereby the heart is filled with desire for His honor; and love to the lost, that longs for their safety. It is a work of the Spirit of God, "whom the world cannot receive"; therefore the world can approve of missions only when they go forward with the highest prosperity.

3. Let no friend of missions become discouraged when the work proceeds slowly. Although every baptized person is not converted, although even among the converts there still may be perversity, although some fall back after a profession of faith, remember that your own church is far from perfect. Among our forefathers in Europe, a whole century was occupied with the introduction of Christianity. Let us not expect too much from the heathen at once, but with love and patience and firm faith, pray and work and expect the blessing of God.

CHAPTER 32

Light and Joyfulness

"Blessed is the people that know the joyful sound: they shall walk, O Lord, in the light of thy countenance. In thy name shall they rejoice all the day" (Ps. 89:15, 16).

"Light is sown for the righteous, and gladness for the upright in heart" (Ps. 97:11).

"I am the light of the world: he that followeth me shall not walk in darkness, but shall have the light of life" (John 8:12).

"I will see you again, and your heart shall rejoice, and your joy no one taketh from you" (John 16:22).

"As sorrowful, yet always rejoicing" (2 Cor. 6:10).

A father is always eager to see his children joyful. He does all that he can to make them happy. God also desires that His children should walk before Him in gladness of heart. He has promised them gladness. He will give it.[1] He has commanded it. We must take it and walk in it at all times.[2]

The reason for this is not difficult to find. Gladness is always the symbol that something really satisfies me and has great value for me. More than anything else gladness for what I possess is a recommendation of it to others. And gladness in God is the strongest proof that I do not serve Him with dread, or to be kept, but because He is my salvation. Gladness is the symbol of the truth and the worth of obedi-

---

[1]Ps. 89:16, 17; Isa. 29:19; John 16:22; 1 Pet. 1:8
[2]Ps. 32:11; Isa. 12:5, 6; 1 Thess. 5:16; Phil. 4:4

ence, showing whether I have pleasure in the will of God.[3] It is for this reason that joy in God is so acceptable to Him, so strengthening to believers themselves, and to all who are around the most eloquent testimony of what we think of God.[4]

In the Scriptures light and gladness are frequently connected with each other.[5] It is so in nature. The joyful light of the morning awakens the birds to their song and gladdens the watchers who in the darkness have longed for the day. It is the light of God's countenance that gives the Christian his gladness. In fellowship with his Lord he can, and always will, be happy. The love of the Father shines like the sun upon His children.[6] When darkness comes over the soul, it is always through one of two things—through sin or through unbelief. Sin is darkness and makes dark. And unbelief also makes dark, for it turns us from Him who alone is the light.

The question is sometimes asked, "Can the Christian always walk in the light?" The answer of our Lord is clear: "He that followeth me shall *not* walk in darkness." It is sin, the turning from Jesus to our own way, that makes dark. But the moment we confess sin and have it cleansed in the blood, we are again in the light.[7] Or it is unbelief that makes dark. We look to ourselves and our strength; we seek comfort in our own feeling, or our own works, and all becomes dark. As soon as we look to Jesus—to His fullness, to the perfect provision for our needs that is in Him—all is light. He says, "I am the light: he that followeth me shall not walk in darkness, but shall have the light of life." As long as I believe, I have light and gladness.[8]

Christians who would walk according to the will of the Lord, hear what His Word says: "Finally, my brethren, re-

---

[3]Deut. 28:47; Ps. 9; 119:111

[4]Neh. 8:11; Ps. 68:4; Prov. 4:18

[5]Esther 8:16; Prov. 13:9; 15:30; Isa. 60:20

[6]Ex. 10:23; 2 Sam. 23:4; Ps. 36:10; Isa. 60:1, 20; 1 John 1:5; 4:16

[7]Josh. 7:13; Isa. 58:10; 59:1, 2, 9; Matt. 15:14, 16; 2 Cor. 6:14; Eph. 5:8, 14; 1 Thess. 5:5; 1 John 2:10

[8]John 12:36; 11:40; Rom. 15:13; 1 Pet. 1:3

joice in the Lord. Rejoice in the Lord always: again, I will say, Rejoice."[9] In the Lord Jesus there is joy unspeakable and full of glory. Believing in Him, rejoice in this. Live the life of faith; that life is salvation and glorious joy. A heart that gives itself undividedly to follow Jesus, that lives by faith in Him and His love, shall have light and gladness. Therefore, *only believe.* Do not seek gladness; in that case you will not find it, because you are seeking feeling. But seek Jesus, follow Jesus, believe in Jesus, and gladness will be added to you. "not seeing, but believing, rejoice with joy unspeakable and full of glory."

Lord Jesus, you are the light of the world, the full expression of the unapproachable light, in whom we see the light of God. From your countenance radiates upon us the illumination of the knowledge of the love and glory of God. And you are ours, our light and our salvation. Oh, teach us to believe more firmly that with you we can never walk in the darkness. Let gladness be the proof that you are all to us and our strength to do all that you would have us do. Amen.

1. The gladness that I have in anything is the measure of its worth in my eyes; the gladness in a person, the measure of my pleasure in him; the gladness in a work, the measure of my pleasure in it. Gladness in God and His service is one of the surest signs of healthy spiritual life.

2. Gladness is hindered by *ignorance* when we do not rightly understand God and His love and the blessedness of His service; by *unbelief* when we still seek something in our own strength or feeling; by *double-mindedness* when we are not willing to give up and lay aside everything for Jesus.

3. Understand this saying: "He that seeks gladness shall not find it; he that seeks the Lord and His will shall find gladness unsought." Think about this. He that seeks gladness as a thing of feeling seeks himself; he will not find it. He who forgets himself to live in the Lord and His will shall

---

[9]Phil. 3:1; 4:6

be taught to rejoice in the Lord. It is God, God himself, who is the God of the gladness of our rejoicing. Seek God and you have gladness. You have then simply to take and enjoy it by faith.

4. To thank much for what God is and does, to believe much in what God says and will do, is the way to abiding gladness.

5. "The light of the eyes gladdens the heart." God has not intended that His children should walk in darkness. Satan is the prince of the darkness; God is light. Christ is the light of the world; we are children of light. Let us walk in the light. Let us believe in the promise, "The Lord shall be to thee an everlasting light. Thy sun shall no more go down, for the Lord shall be to thee an everlasting light, and the days of thy mourning shall be ended."

CHAPTER 33

Chastisement

"Blessed is the man whom thou chasteneth, O Lord, and teachest him out of thy law; that thou mayest give him rest from the days of adversity" (Ps. 94:12).

"Before I was afflicted I went astray; but now have I kept thy word. It is good for me that I have been afflicted; that I might learn thy statutes" (Ps. 119:67, 71).

"He [chastens us] for our profit, that we might be partakers of his holiness" (Heb. 12:10).

"Count it all joy, when ye fall into divers temptations; knowing this that the trying of your faith worketh patience" (James 1:2, 3).

Every believer must at some time enter the school of trial. What the Scriptures teach us is confirmed by experience. And the Scriptures teach us further that we are to count it a joy when God takes us into this school. It is a part of our heavenly blessedness to be educated and sanctified by the Father through chastisement.

Not that trial in itself brings a blessing.[1] Just as there is no profit in the ground's being made wet by rain or broken up by the plow when no seed is planted into it, so there are children of God who enter into trial and receive little blessing from it. The heart is softened for a time, but they do not obtain an abiding blessing from it. They do not understand what the Father has in view for them in the school of trial.

In a good school there are four things necessary: a definite

---

[1] Isa. 5:3; Hos. 7:14, 15; 2 Cor. 7:10

goal, a good textbook, a capable teacher, a willing pupil.

1. *Let the goal of trial be clear to you.* Holiness is the highest glory of the Father and also of the believer. He chastens us "for our profit, that we might be partakers of *his holiness*."[2] In trial the believer often only wants relief. Or he seeks to be quiet and contented under the special chastisement. This is indeed the beginning; but the Father desires something else, something higher. He would make him *holy*, for his whole life. When Job said, "Blessed be the name of the Lord," this was but the beginning of his schooltime; the Lord had still more to teach him. God desires to unite our will with His holy will not only on the one point in which He is trying us but in everything. God would fill us with His Holy Spirit, with His holiness. This is the goal of God; this also must be your goal in the school of trial.

2. *Let the Word of God at this time be your reading book.* See in our trials how in affliction God would teach us out of His Word. The Word will reveal to you why the Father chastens you, how deeply He loves you in the midst of it, and how rich are the promises of His consolation. Trial will give new glory to the promises of the Father. In chastisement go to the Word for strength.[3]

3. *Let Jesus be your teacher.* He himself was sanctified by suffering; it was in suffering that He learned full obedience. He has a wonderfully sympathetic heart. Spend time in communion with Him. Do not try to receive your comfort from others. *Give Jesus the opportunity of teaching you.* Have fellowship with Him in solitude.[4] The Father has given you the Word, the Spirit, the Lord Jesus as your sanctification in order to sanctify you; affliction and chastisement are meant to bring you to the Word, to Jesus himself, in order that He may make you a partaker of His holiness. It is in fellowship with Jesus that consolation comes as of itself.[5]

---

[2] Isa. 27:8, 9; 1 Cor. 11:32; Heb. 2:10; 12:11

[3] Ps. 119:49, 50, 92, 143; Isa. 40:1; 43:2; Heb. 12:10–13

[4] Isa. 26:16; 61:1, 2; Heb. 2:10, 17, 18; 5:9

[5] 2 Cor. 1:3, 4; Heb. 13:5, 6

4. *Be a willing pupil.* Acknowledge your ignorance. Think not that you understand the will of God. Ask and expect that the Lord would teach you the lesson that you are to learn in affliction. To the meek there is the promise of teaching and wisdom. Seek to have the ear open, the heart very quiet and turned toward God. Know that it is the Father who has placed you in the school of trial; yield yourself with all willingness to hear what He says, to learn what He would teach you. He will bless you greatly in this.[6]

"Blessed is the man whom thou chasteneth . . . and teachest him out of thy law." "Count it all joy when ye fall into divers temptations . . . that ye may be perfect, lacking nothing." Regard the time of trial as a time of blessing, as a time of close fellowship with the Father, of being made a partaker of His holiness; and you shall also rejoicingly say, "It is good for me that I have been afflicted."

Father, what thanks shall I express to you for the glorious light that your Word casts upon the dark trials of this life. You will teach me and make me a partaker of your holiness. You considered the suffering and the death of your beloved Son not too much to bring holiness near to me, and shall I not be willing to endure your chastisement to be a partaker of it? No, Father, thanks be unto you for your precious work; only fulfill your counsel in me. Amen.

1. In chastisement it is first of all necessary that we should be possessed by the thought: This is the will of God. Although the trial may come through our own folly or the perversity of men, we must acknowledge that it is the will of God that we should be in that suffering. We see this clearly in Joseph and the Lord Jesus. Nothing will give us rest but the willing acknowledgment that this is the will of God.

2. The second thought is this: God wills not only the trial but also the consolation, the power, and the blessing in it. He who acknowledges the will of God in the chastisement

---

[6]Ps. 25:9; 39:2, 10; Isa. 50:4, 5

itself is on the way to seeing and experiencing the accompaniments also as the will of God.

3. The will of God is as perfect as He himself is; let us not be afraid to surrender ourselves to it. No one suffers loss by deeming the will of God unconditionally good.

4. This is holiness: to know and to adore the will of God, to unite one's self wholly with it.

5. Do not seek comfort in your trial through men. Do not mingle too much with them; see to it rather that you deal with God and His Word. *The object of trial is to draw you away from what is earthly in order that you may turn to God and give Him time to unite your will with His perfect will.*

CHAPTER 34

Prayer

"Thou, when thou prayest, enter into thy closet, and when thou hast shut thy door, pray to the Father which is in secret, and thy Father which seeth in secret shall reward thee openly" (Matt. 6:6).

The growth of our spiritual life depends in great measure on prayer. According as I pray much or little, pray with pleasure or as a duty, pray according to the Word of God or my own inclination—so will my life flourish or decay. In the words of Jesus quoted above, we have the primary ideas of true prayer.

Alone with God—that is the first thought. The door must be shut, with the world and man outside, because I am to have fellowship with God undisturbed. When God met with His servants in the olden time, He took them alone.[1] Let the first thought in your prayer be: God and I are in this room with each other. According to your conviction of the nearness of God will be the power of your prayer.

In the presence of your Father—this is the second thought. You come to the inner room, because your Father with His love awaits you there. Although you may sense your own coldness and darkness, although you may doubt whether you can pray at all—come, because the Father is there and there looks upon you. Set yourself beneath the light of His eye.

---

[1] Gen. 18:22, 23; 22:5; 32:24; Ex. 33:11

134

Believe in His tender, fatherly love, and out of this faith prayer will be born.[2]

Count upon an answer—that is the third point in the words of Jesus. "Your Father will reward you openly." There is nothing about which the Lord Jesus has spoken so positively as the certainty of an answer to prayer. Review the promises.[3] Observe how constantly in the Psalms, that prayer book of God's saints, God is called upon as the God who hears prayer and gives answers.[4]

It may be that there is much in you that prevents the answer. Delay in the answer is a very blessed discipline. It leads to self-searching as to whether we are praying incorrectly and whether our life is truly in harmony with our prayer. It rouses to a purer exercise of faith.[5] It leads to a closer and more persistent communion with God. The sure confidence of an answer is the secret of powerful praying. With us, let this always be the chief thing in prayer. When you pray, stop in the midst of your prayer to ask, "Do I believe that I am receiving what I pray for?" Let your faith receive and hold fast the answer as given; it will occur according to your faith.[6]

Beloved new believers, if there is one thing about which you must be conscientious, it is this: private communion with God. Your life is hid with Christ in God. Every day you must, in prayer, ask from above and by faith receive in prayer what you need for that day. Every day personal communion with the Father and the Lord Jesus must be renewed and strengthened. God is our salvation and our strength. Christ is our life and holiness. Only in personal fellowship with the living God is our blessedness found.

---

[2] Matt. 6:8; 7:11

[3] Matt. 6:7, 8; Mark 11:24; Luke 18:8; John 14:13, 14; 15:7, 16; 16:23, 24

[4] Ps. 3:4; 4:3; 6:9; 10:17; 17:6; 20:2, 7; 34:5, 7, 17, 18; 38:15; 40:1, 2; 65:2; 66:19

[5] Josh. 7:12; 1 Sam. 8:18; 14:37, 38; 28:6, 15; Prov. 21:13; Isa. 1:15; Mic. 3:4; Hag. 1:9; James 1:6; 4:3; 5:16

[6] Ps. 145:9; Isa. 30:19; Jer. 33:3; Mal. 3:10; Matt. 9:29; 15:28; 1 John 3:22; 5:14, 15

Believer, pray much, pray continually, pray without ceasing. When you have no desire to pray, *go just then to the inner chamber.* Go as one who has nothing to bring to the Father, to set yourself before Him in faith in His love; that coming to the Father and abiding before Him is already a prayer that He understands. Be assured that to appear before God, however passively, always brings a blessing. The Father not only hears; He sees in secret and will reward it openly.

O my Father, you have so clearly promised in your Word to hear the prayer of faith, give to me the Spirit of prayer that I may know how to offer that prayer. Graciously reveal to me your wonderful fatherly love, the complete blotting out of my sins in Christ, by which every hindrance in this direction is taken away; and reveal the intercession of the Spirit in me, by which my ignorance or weakness cannot deprive me of the blessing. Teach me to pray in fellowship with you. And confirm in me the strong certainty that I receive what I believingly ask for. Amen.

1. In prayer the most essential element is faith. The whole of salvation, the whole of the new life, is by faith and therefore also by prayer. There is far too much prayer that brings nothing, because there is little faith in it. Before I pray, and while I pray, and after I have prayed, I must ask: Do I pray in faith? I must say, I believe with my whole heart.

2. To arrive at this faith we must take time in prayer—time to set ourselves silently and trustfully before God and to be refreshed in His presence; time to have our soul sanctified in fellowship with God; time for the Holy Spirit to teach us to hold fast and use trustfully the word of promise. We do not gain earthly knowledge, possessions, food, or fellowship with friends, without it taking time. We should not expect to learn how to pray, how to enjoy the power and the blessedness of prayer, if we do not take time with God.

3. And then there must be not only time every day but perseverance from day to day. Time is required to grow in

the certainty that we are acceptable to the Father and that our prayer has power, in the confidence which knows that our prayer is according to His will and is heard. Prayer is conversation and fellowship with God in which God has time and opportunity to work in us; in which our souls die to their own will and power and become bound up and united with God.

4. For encouragement in persistent prayer, the following example may be of help. George Müller said that in 1844 five persons were laid upon his heart, and that he began to pray for their conversion. Eighteen months passed before the first was converted. He prayed for five more years, when the second was converted. After twelve and a half years, yet another was converted. And now he has already prayed forty years for the other two, without letting it slip a single day; and still they are not converted. He was, nevertheless, full of confidence that these two also would be given him in answer to his prayer. This is a confident prayer life.

CHAPTER 35

The Prayer Meeting

"Again I say unto you, That if two of you shall agree on earth as touching any thing that they shall ask, it shall be done for them of my Father which is in heaven. For where two or three are gathered together in my name, there am I in the midst of them" (Matt. 18:19, 20).

Jesus told us to go into the inner chamber and hold our personal conversation with God in secret and not to be seen by men. The very same voice tells us that we are also to pray in fellowship with one another.[1] When He went to heaven, the birth of the Christian Church took place in a prayer meeting which one hundred and twenty men and women held for ten days.[2] The Day of Pentecost was the fruit of unanimous persevering prayer. Let everyone who would please the Lord Jesus, who desires the gift of the Spirit with power for his church, who would have the blessing of fellowship with the children of God, attach himself to a prayer meeting and prove whether the Lord will make good His Word and bestow upon it a special blessing.[3] And let him actively participate in it, so that the prayer meeting may be what the Lord desires it to be.

For a prayer meeting to be effective, there must be, first of all, agreement concerning the thing which we desire. There must be something that we really desire to have from God,

---

[1]Matt. 6:6; Luke 9:18, 28
[2]Acts 1:14
[3]2 Chron. 20:4, 17, 18; Neh. 9:2, 3; Joel 2:16, 17; Acts 12:5

and concerning this we are to be in harmony. There must be inner love and unity among the members—all that is strife, envy, wrath, lovelessness, makes powerless[4]—and then agreement on the definite object that is desired.[5] To reach this goal it is entirely proper that the people should be told what to pray for in the prayer meeting. Whether it be that one of the members would have his particular needs met, or whether others would bring more general needs to the Lord, such as the conversion of the lost, the revival of God's children, the anointing of the teacher, the extension of the kingdom—let the goals be announced beforehand. Do not assume that there is unanimity whenever one is content to join in prayer for these objects. No, we are to take them into our heart and life, bring them continually before the Lord, be inwardly eager that the Lord should give them; then we are on the way to the prayer that has power.

The second feature that characterizes an effective prayer meeting is the coming together in the name of Jesus and the consciousness of His presence. The Scripture says, "The name of the Lord is a strong tower: the righteous runneth into it, and is safe."[6] The name is the expression of the person. When they come together, believers are to enter into the name of Jesus, to take upon themselves this name as their fortress and abode.

In this name they abide with one another before the Father, and out of this name they pray; this name makes them truly one with each other. And when they are in this name, the living Lord is in their midst! and He says that this is the reason why the Father certainly hears them.[7] They are in Him and He is in them, and out of Him they pray, and their prayer comes before the Father in His power. Oh, let the name of Jesus be the point of union, the meeting place, in our prayer meetings, and we shall be conscious that He is in our midst.

---

[4]Ps. 133:1, 3; Jer. 50:4, 5; Matt. 5:23, 24; 18:19, 20; Mark 11:25
[5]Jer. 32:39; Acts 4:24
[6]Prov. 18:10
[7]John 14:13, 14; 15:7, 16; 16:23, 24

Then there is the third feature of united prayer of which the Lord has told us: our request shall be accomplished by the heavenly Father. The prayer shall certainly be answered. We may well cry out in these days, "Where is the God of Elijah?" for He was a God that answered. "The God that shall answer, he shall be God," said Elijah to the people. And he said to God, "Answer me, Lord; answer me; that this people may acknowledge that thou, O Lord, art God."[8]

When we are content with praying without answer, then there will be little answer given. But when we understand that the answer is the expression of God's pleasure in our prayer and we will not be content without it, we will discover what is lacking in our prayer and will set ourselves so to pray that an answer may come. We should believe this: the Lord takes delight in answering. It is a joy to Him when His people so enter into the name of Jesus, and pray out of it, that He can give what they desire.[9]

New believers, however young and weak you may be, the prayer meeting is one of God's institutions prepared to supply you with help in prayer. Let everyone make use of the prayer meeting. Let everyone go in a praying and believing frame of mind, seeking the name and the presence of the Lord. Let everyone seek to live and pray with other believers. And let everyone expect to see glorious answers to prayer.

Blessed Lord Jesus, you who have told us to pray in private as well as in public fellowship with one another, let the one habit always make the other more precious as the complement and confirmation. Let the inner chamber prepare us and awaken the need for union with your people in prayer. Let your presence there be our blessedness. And let fellowship with your people strengthen us to expect and receive answers. Amen.

1. There are many places where prayer meetings are

---

[8] 1 Kings 18:24, 37; James 5:16
[9] Acts 12:5; 2 Cor. 1:11; James 4:3; 5:16, 17

needed. Let every believing reader inquire if there does not exist in his neighborhood some such need, and let him make such a beginning in the name of the Lord. Let me put the question to every reader: Is there a prayer meeting in your area? Do you faithfully take part in it? Do you know what it is to come together with the children of God in the name of Jesus to experience His presence and His hearing of prayer?

2. You may want to use this book as a starting point for discussion and then prayer. A chapter could be read, and some of the texts reviewed and spoken upon. This will give material for prayer.

3. Will the prayer meeting do no harm to the inner chamber? is a question sometimes asked. My experience is just the reverse of this result. The prayer meeting is a school of prayer. The weak learn from more advanced members. Material for prayer is given; there is opportunity for self-searching and encouragement to more prayer.

4. Remember to ask for people to speak of definite objects for which to pray, things for which one can definitely and trustfully expect an answer and concerning which one can know when an answer comes. Such announcements would greatly further unanimity and believing expectation.

CHAPTER 36

The Fear of the Lord

"Blessed is the man that feareth the Lord. . . . He shall not be afraid of evil tidings. . . . . His heart is established, he shall not be afraid" (Ps. 112:1, 7, 8).

"The churches . . . walking in the fear of the Lord and in the comfort of the Holy Ghost, were multiplied" (Acts 9:31).

The Scriptures use the word "fear" in a twofold way. In some places it speaks of fear as something wrong and sinful, and in the strongest terms forbids us to fear.[1] The words "fear not" occur in nearly one hundred places. In many other places, fear is praised as one of the true expressions of godliness, acceptable to the Lord, and fruitful of blessing to us.[2] The people of God bear the name "those that fear the Lord." The distinction between these two lies in this simple fact: the one is unbelieving fear, the other is believing.

Where fear is connected with lack of trust in God, there it is sinful and very harmful.[3] The fear, on the other hand, that is coupled with trust and hope in God is entirely indispensable for the spiritual life. The fear that has man and what is temporal for its object is condemned. The fear that with childlike confidence and love honors the Father is commanded.[4] It is the believing, not slavish but childlike, fear of the Lord that is presented in the Scriptures as a source of

---

[1]Gen. 15:1; Isa. 8:13; Jer. 32:40; Rom. 8:15; 1 Pet. 3:14; 1 John 4:18
[2]Ps. 22:23, 25; 33:18; 112:1; 115:13; Prov. 28:14
[3]Matt. 8:26; Rev. 21:8
[4]Ps. 33:18; 147:11; Luke 12:4, 7

blessing and power. He that fears the Lord will fear nothing else. The fear of the Lord will be the beginning of all wisdom. The fear of the Lord is the sure way to the enjoyment of God's favor and protection.[5]

There are some believers who by their upbringing are led into the fear of the Lord even before they come to faith. This is a great blessing. Parents can give a child no greater blessing than to bring him up in the fear of the Lord. When these are brought to faith, they have a great advantage: they are, as it were, prepared to walk in the joy of the Lord. When, on the contrary, others who have not this preparation come to conversion, they have need of special teaching and vigilance in order to pray for and awaken this holy fear.

The characteristics of which this fear is composed are many. The principal are the following:

Holy reverence and awe before the glorious majesty of God and before the All Holy. These guard against the superficiality that forgets who God is and that takes no pains to honor Him as God.[6]

Deep humility that is afraid of itself and couples deep confidence in God with an entire distrust in itself. Conscious weakness that knows the subtlety of its own heart always dreads doing anything contrary to the will or honor of God. Because he fears God, such a one firmly depends on Him for protection. And this same humility inspires him in all his communication with his fellowmen.[7]

Cautiousness or vigilance. With holy forethought, it seeks to know the right path, to watch against the enemy, and to be guarded against all lightness or hastiness in speech, decisions, and conduct.[8]

Holy zeal and courage in watching and striving. The fear of displeasing the Lord by not conducting oneself in everything as His servant incites to being faithful in that which

---

[5]Ps. 56:4, 11; Prov. 1:7; 9:10; 10:27; 19:23; Acts 9:31; 2 Cor. 7:1

[6]Job 42:6; Ps. 5:7; Isa. 6:3, 5; Hab. 2:20; Zeph. 2:3

[7]Luke 18:2, 4; Rom. 11:20; 1 Pet. 3:2, 5

[8]Prov. 2:5, 11; 8:12, 13; 13:13; 16:6; Luke 1:74

is least. The fear of the Lord takes all other fear away and gives inconceivable courage in the certainty of victory.[9]

And out of this fear is then born joy. "Rejoice with trembling." The fear of the Lord gives joy its depth and stability. Fear is the root, joy the fruit; the deeper the fear, the greater the joy. On this account it is said, "Ye that fear the Lord, praise him"; "Ye that fear the Lord, bless the Lord."[10]

New believers, hear the voice of your Father. "Fear the Lord, ye his saints." Let deep fear of the Lord and dread of all that might displease or grieve Him fill you. Then you will never have any evil to fear. It is for those who fear the Lord and seek to do all that pleases Him that God also does all they desire. The childlike believing fear of God will lead you into the love and joy of God, while slavish, unbelieving, cowardly fear is utterly cast out.

O my God, unite my heart to fear your name. May I always be among those who fear the Lord, who hope in His mercy. Amen.

1. What are some of the blessings of the fear of God? (Ps. 31:20; 115:13; 127:11; 45:19; Prov. 1; 7; 8; 13; 14; 27; Acts 10:35).

2. What are the reasons we are to fear God? (Deut. 10:17, 20, 21; Josh. 4:24; 1 Sam. 12:24; Jer. 5:22; 10:6, 7; Matt. 10:28; Rev. 15:4).

3. It is especially the knowledge of God in His greatness, power, and glory that will fill the soul with fear. But for this end we must set ourselves silently before Him and take time for our soul to come under the impression of His majesty.

4. "He delivered me from all my fears." Does this apply to every sort of fear by which you are hindered? There is the fear of man (Isa. 2:12, 13; Heb. 13:16); the fear of heavy trial (Isa. 40:1, 2); the fear of our own weakness (Isa. 12:10); fear

---

[9]Deut. 6:2; Isa. 12:2
[10]Ps. 22:23; 135:20

for the work of God (1 Chron. 28:20); the fear of death (Ps. 23:4).

5. Do you now understand the word, "Blessed is the man that fears the Lord. His heart is established, he shall not be afraid"?

CHAPTER 37

Undivided Consecration

*"And Ittai answered, . . . As the Lord liveth . . . surely in
what place my lord the king shall be, whether in death or life,
even there also will thy servant be"* (2 Sam. 15:21).

*"Whosoever he be of you that forsaketh not all that he hath,
he cannot be my disciple"* (Luke 14:33).

*"Come out from among them, and be ye separate, saith the
Lord, and touch not the unclean thing; and I will receive you,
and will be a Father unto you"* (2 Cor. 6:17, 18).

*"Yea doubtless, and I count all things but loss for . . . Christ
Jesus my Lord"* (Phil. 3:8).

We have already said that surrender to the Lord is something that always obtains newer and deeper significance for
the Christian. He comes to understand how this surrender
involves nothing less than a complete and undivided consecration to live only, always, wholly for Jesus. As entirely as
the temple was dedicated to the service of God alone, so that
everyone knew that it existed only for that purpose; as entirely as the offering on the altar could be used only according to the command of God, and no one had a right to dispose
of one portion of it other than as God had said—so entirely
do you belong to your Lord, and so undivided must your consecration be to Him. God continually reminded Israel that
He had redeemed them to be His possession.[1] Let us see what
this implied.

There is *personal attachment to Jesus* and communion

---

[1]Ex. 19:4, 5; Lev. 1:8, 9; Deut. 7:6; Rom. 12:1; 1 Cor. 3:16, 17

with Him in private. He will be, He must be, the beloved, the desire, the joy of our souls. It is not to the service of God but to Jesus as our Friend and King, our Redeemer and God, that we are to be consecrated.[2] It is only the spiritual impulse of a personal cordial love that can place us in a condition for a life of complete consecration. Jesus continually used the words: "For my sake," "Follow me," "My disciple." He must be the central point.[3] He gave himself; to desire to have Him, to love, to depend on Him is the characteristic of a disciple.

Then there is *public confession*. What has been given to anyone, that he will have acknowledged by all as his property. His possessions are his glory. When the Lord Jesus manifests His great grace to a soul in redeeming it, He desires that the world should see and know it. He would be known and honored as its owner. He desires that everyone who belongs to Him should confess Him as King.[4] Apart from this public confession, the surrender is but a halfhearted one.

As a part of this public confession, it is also required that we should join His people and acknowledge them as our people. The one new commandment that the Lord gave, the expression by which all should recognize that we are His disciples, is brotherly love. Although the children of God in a locality may be few, or despised, or full of imperfection, yet you must join them. Love them; fellowship with them; attach yourself to them in prayer meetings and otherwise. Love them fervently; brotherly love has wonderful power to open the heart for the love and the indwelling of God.[5]

To complete consecration, there also belongs separation from sin and the world. Touch not the unclean thing. Know that the world is under the power of the evil one. Ask not how much of it you can retain without being lost. Ask not what is sin and what is lawful. Even of that which is lawful, the Christian must oftentimes make a willing renunciation

---

[2]John 14:21; 15:14, 15; 21:17; Gal. 2:20

[3]Matt. 10:32, 33, 37, 38, 40; Luke 14:26, 27, 33; 18:22

[4]Ex. 33:16; Josh. 24:15; John 8:35

[5]Ruth 1:16; John 15:12; Rom. 12:5; 1 Cor. 12:20, 21; Eph. 4:14, 16; 1 Pet. 1:22

in order to be able to live wholly for his God.[6] Abstinence even from lawful things is often indispensable for the full imitation of the Lord Jesus. Live as one who is really separated to God and His holiness. He who renounces everything, who counts everything but loss for Jesus' sake, shall even in this life receive a hundredfold.[7]

And what I separate from everything, I will use. Entire consecration has its eye upon making us useful and fit for God and His service. Have no doubt as to whether God has need of you and will make you a great blessing. Only give yourself unreservedly into His hands. Present yourself to Him that He may fill you with His blessing, His love, His Spirit. You shall be a blessing.[8]

Let no one fear that this demand for a complete consecration is too much for him. You are not under the law which demands but gives no power. You are under grace which works what it requires.[9] Like the first surrender, so is every fresh dedication yielded to this Jesus whom the Father has given to do all things for you. Consecration is a work of faith, a part of the glorious life of faith. It is on this account that you have to say, "It is not I but the grace of God in me that will do it. I live only by faith in Him who works in me the willing as well as the performance."[10]

Blessed Lord, open the eyes of my heart that I may see how completely you would have me for yourself. Be in the hidden depths of my heart the one power that keeps me occupied and holds me in possession. Let everyone know that you are my King, that I ask only for your will. In my separation from the world, in my surrender to your people and to your will, let it be manifest that I am wholly, yea, wholly, the Lord's. Amen.

1. There is no point of the Christian life which I should

---

[6]1 Cor. 8:13; 9:25, 27; 10:23; 2 Cor. 6:16, 17; 2 Tim. 2:4
[7]Gen. 22:13, 17; 2 Chron. 25:9; Luke 18:29, 30; John 12:24, 25; Phil. 3:8
[8]2 Tim. 2:21
[9]2 Cor. 9:8; 2 Thess. 1:11, 12
[10]1 Cor. 15:10; Gal. 2:20; Phil. 2:13

more desire that God might enlighten your eyes to see than the entire consecration that He desires. In myself and others, I discover that with our own thoughts we cannot conceive of how completely God would take possession of our will and live in us. The Holy Spirit must reveal this in us. Only then does a conviction arise of how little we understand this. We are not to think, "I see how entirely I should live for God, but I cannot accomplish this." No, we are to say, "I am still blind. I still have not seen the glory of a life in which God is all." If I saw it, I would strongly desire and believe that only God can work it in me.

2. There should not be in your mind the least doubt as to whether you have given yourself to God to live wholly and only as His. Express this conviction often before Him. Acknowledge that you do not yet see or understand what it means, but abide by this, that you desire it to be so. Depend on the Holy Spirit to seal you, to stamp you as God's entire possession. Even if you stumble and discover self-will, hold fast your integrity, and reaffirm that the deep, firm choice of your heart is in all things to live to God.

3. Always keep before your eyes that the power of dedication to the Lord and to be all for the Lord arises from the fact that He has given all for you, that He is all for you. Faith in what He did for you is the power of what you do for Him.

CHAPTER 38

Assurance of Faith

"He [Abraham] staggered not at the promise of God through unbelief, but was strong in faith, giving glory to God; and being fully persuaded that, what he had promised, he was able also to perform" (Rom. 4:20, 21).

"My little children, let us not love in word, neither in tongue; but in deed and truth. And hereby we know that we are of the truth, and shall assure our hearts before him" (1 John 3:18, 19).

"And hereby we know that he abideth in us, by the Spirit which he hath given us" (1 John 3:24).

Every believer has need of the assurance of faith—the full certainty of faith that the Lord has received him and made him His child. The Scriptures always speak to believers as those that know that they are redeemed, that they are children of God, and that they have received eternal life.[1] How can a child love or serve his father while he is uncertain whether his father will really acknowledge him as his child? We have already spoken about this in a previous chapter; but sometimes through ignorance or distrust a Christian again comes into darkness. For this reason we will deal with it again.

Scripture names three things by which we can have our assurance: first, *faith* in the Word; after that, *works*; and then, in and with both of these, *the Holy Spirit*.

First, *faith in the Word*. Abraham is to us the great ex-

---

[1]Deut. 26:17, 18; Isa. 44:5; Gal. 4:7; 1 John 5:12

ample of faith and also of the assurance of faith. What does the Scripture say about the certainty that he had? He was fully assured that what God had promised He was also able to perform. His expectation was only from God and what God had promised. He relied upon God to do what He had said. The promise of God was his only, but sufficient, assurance of faith.[2]

There are many new believers who think that faith in the Word is not sufficient; they want something more. They imagine that assurance, a sure inward feeling or conviction, is what is given above or outside of faith. This is wrong. As I have need of nothing more than the word of a trustworthy man to give me complete confidence, so must the Word of God be my certainty. People err when they seek something in themselves and in their felings. No, the whole of salvation comes from God; the soul must not be occupied with itself or its work but with God. He that forgets himself to hear what God says and to rely upon His promise as something worthy of credit has in this fact the fullest assurance of faith.[3] He does not doubt the promise, but is strong in faith, giving God the glory and being fully assured that what was promised, God is also able to perform.

Then the Scripture also mentions *works*. By genuine love that does works we shall assure our hearts.[4] Carefully observe this: assurance by faith in the promise, without works, comes first. The godless man who receives grace knows this only from the Word. But then, later on, assurance is to follow from works. "By works was faith made perfect."[5] The tree is planted in faith without fruits. But when the time of fruit arrives, and no fruit appears, then I may doubt. If at the outset, I hold the assurance of faith, without works, on the Word alone, the more certainly shall works follow.

And both—assurance by faith and by works—come by the

---

[2]John 3:33; 5:24; Acts 27:25; Rom. 4:21, 22; 1 John 5:10, 11

[3]Num. 23:19; Ps. 89:35; Isa. 54:9

[4]1 John 3:18, 19

[5]John 15:10, 14; Gal. 5:6; James 2:22; 1 John 3:14

Spirit. Not by the Word alone, and not by works as something that I myself do, but by the Word as the instrument of the Spirit and by works as the fruit of the Spirit has a child of God the heavenly certification that he is the Lord's.[6]

Oh, let us believe in Jesus as our life and abide in Him, and assurance of faith shall never be lacking to us.

O my Father, teach me to know my assurance of faith in a life with you, in loving reliance upon your promises, and in loving obedience to your commands. Let your Holy Spirit also witness with my spirit that I am a child of God. Amen.

1. The importance of the assurance of faith lies in the fact that, childlike, I cannot possibly love or serve God if I do not know He loves and acknowledges me as His child.

2. The whole Bible is one great proof for the assurance of faith. Abraham and Moses knew very well that God had received them; otherwise they could not serve or trust Him. Israel knew that God had redeemed them; for this reason they had to serve God. How much more must this be the case in the greater redemption of the New Testament? All the Epistles were written to men who knew and confessed that they are redeemed, holy children of God.

3. Faith and obedience are inseparable, as root and fruit. First, there must be the root, and the root must have time without fruits; then later on come the fruits—first assurance without fruits by living faith in the Word; then further assurance from fruits. It is in a life with Jesus that assurance of faith is exalted firmly above all doubt.

4. Assurance of faith is helped by confession. What I express becomes for me more evident; I am bound and confirmed by it.

5. It is at the feet of Jesus, looking up into His lovely face, listening to His promises and communing with Him in prayer, that all doubtfulness of mind falls away. In His presence is the full assurance of faith.

---

[6]John 4:13; Rom. 8:13, 14; 1 John 3:24

CHAPTER 39

Conformity to Jesus

"Predestinated to be conformed to the image of his Son" (Rom. 8:29).
"I have given you an example, that ye should do as I have done to you" (John 13:15).

The Bible speaks of a twofold conformity, a twofold likeness that we bear. We may be conformed to the world or to Jesus. The one excludes and drives out the other. Conformity to Jesus, where it is sought, is prevented by conformity to the world more than anything else. And conformity to the world can be overcome by nothing but conformity to Jesus.

New believer, the new life of which you have become a partaker is the life of God in heaven. In Christ that life is revealed and made visible. What the workings and fruits of eternal life were in Jesus, they shall also be in you. In His life you see what eternal life will work in you. It cannot be otherwise. If for this end you surrender yourself unreservedly to Jesus and the dominion of eternal life, it will bring forth in you a walk of wonderful conformity to Jesus.[1]

To the true imitation of Jesus in His example, and growth in inward conformity to Him, two things are especially necessary. These are *a clear insight* that I am really called to this and *a firm trust* that it is possible for me.

One of the greatest hindrances to spiritual life is that we do not know, that we do not see, what God desires us to be.[2]

---

[1]Matt. 20:27, 28; Luke 6:40; John 6:57; 1 John 2:6; 4:17
[2]Luke 24:16; 1 Cor. 3:1, 2; Heb. 5:11, 12

Our understanding is still so little enlightened, we still have many of our own human thoughts and imaginations about the true service of God, we know so little of waiting for the Spirit who alone can teach us. We do not acknowledge that even the clearest words of God do not have for us the meaning and power that God desires. And as long as we do not spiritually discern what conformity to Jesus is and how fully we are called to live like Him, there can be but little said of true conformity. Our need is that of a special heavenly instruction on this point.[3]

Let us earnestly examine the Scriptures in order to know what God says and desires about our conformity to Christ.[4] Let us unceasingly ponder such words of Scripture and keep our heart in contact with them. Let it remain fixed with us that we have given ourselves wholly to the Lord to be all that He desires. And let us trustfully pray that the Holy Spirit would inwardly enlighten us and bring us to a full view of the life that Jesus can work in a believer.[5] The Spirit will convince us that we, no less than Jesus, are called to live only for the will and glory of the Father—to be in the world even as He is.

The other thing we have need of is the belief that it is really possible for us with some measure of exactness to bear the image of the Lord. Unbelief is the cause of impotence. Because we are powerless, we think we cannot believe that we can be conformed to our Lord. This thought is in conflict with the Word of God. We do not have it in our own power to carry ourselves after the image of Jesus. No, He is our head and our life. He dwells in us and will have His life work from within outwards, with divine power, through the Holy Spirit.[6]

Yet this cannot be apart from our faith. Faith is the consent of the heart, the surrender to Him to work, the reception

---

[3]1 Cor. 2:12, 13; Eph. 1:17–20
[4]John 13:15; 15:10, 12; 17:18; Eph. 5:2; Phil. 2:5; Col. 3:13
[5]1 Cor. 11:1; 2 Cor. 3:18
[6]John 14:23; 2 Cor. 13:3; Eph. 3:17, 18

154

of His working. "Be it unto you according to your faith" is one of the fundamental laws of the kingdom of God.[7] It is incredible what a power unbelief has in hindering the working and the blessing of the Almighty God. The Christian who would be a partaker of conformity to Christ must firmly trust that this blessing is within his reach, is entirely within the range of possibility. He must learn to look to Jesus as the One to whom he can, in his measure, be really conformable. He must believe that the same Spriit that was in Jesus is also in him; that the same Father that led and strengthened Jesus also watches over him; that the same Jesus that lived on earth now lives in him. He must cherish the strong assurance that God is at work in changing him into the image of the Son.[8]

He that believes this shall receive it. It will not be without much prayer; it will require ceaseless communion with God and Jesus. Yet he that desires it and is willing to give time and sacrifice to it certainly receives it.

Son of God, effulgence of the glory of God, the very image of His substance, I must be changed into your image. In you I see the image and the likeness of God in which we are created, in which we are created anew. Lord Jesus, let conformity to yourself be the one desire, the one hope of my soul. Amen.

1. Conformity to Jesus—we think that we understand the word, but how little do we comprehend that God really expects we should live like Jesus. It requires much time with Him, in prayer and pondering of His example, to begin to conceive of it. I have written a book on this theme and often spoken of it; and yet I sometimes feel as if I must cry out, "Is it really true? Has God indeed called us to live like Jesus?"

2. Conformity to the world is strengthened by fellowship with it. It is in fellowship with Jesus where we will adopt His mode of thinking, His disposition, His manners.

[7]Zech. 1:6; Matt. 18:19; Luke 1:37, 45; 18:27; Gal. 2:20
[8]John 14:20; 17:19; Rom. 8:2; 2 Cor. 3:18; Eph. 1:19

3. The chief feature of the life of Jesus is this: He surrendered himself wholly to the Father in behalf of men. This is the chief feature of conformity to Him: the offering up of ourselves to God for the redemption and blessing of the lost.

4. The chief feature of His inner disposition was childlikeness—absolute dependence on the Father, great willingness to be taught, cheerful preparedness to do the will of the Father. Be especially like Him in this.

CHAPTER 40

Conformity to the World

*"I beseech you . . . brethren . . . that ye present your bodies
a living sacrifice, holy, acceptable unto God. . . . And be not
conformed to this world: but be ye transformed by the renewing of your mind, that ye may prove what is that good, and
acceptable, and perfect, will of God"* (Rom. 12:1, 2).

Be not conformed to this world. But what is conformity
to the world? The opposite of conformity to Jesus, for Jesus
and the world stand directly opposed to each other. The world
crucified Him. He and His disciples are not of the world. The
spirit of this world and the Spirit of God exclude each other;
the world cannot receive the Spirit of God, for it sees Him
not and knows Him not.[1]

And what is the spirit of this world? The spirit of this
world is the disposition that animates mankind in their natural condition, where the Spirit of God has not yet renewed
them. The spirit of this world comes from the evil one, who
is the prince of this world and has dominion over all that are
not renewed by the Spirit of God.[2]

And in what does the spirit of this world, or conformity
to it, manifest itself? The Word of God gives the answer: "All
that is in the world, the lust of the flesh, and the lust of the
eyes, and the vainglory of life, is not of the Father, but is of
the world." The craving for pleasure or the desire to enjoy
the world; the craving for property, or the desire to possess

---

[1]John 14:17; 17:14, 16; 1 Cor. 2:6, 8
[2]John 14:30; 16:11; 1 Cor. 2:12

the world; the craving for glory, or the desire to be honored in the world—these are the three chief forms of the spirit of the world.[3]

These three are one in root and essence. The spirit of this world is that man makes himself his own end; he makes himself the central point in the world. All creation, as far as he has power over it, must serve him; he seeks his life in the visible. This is the spirit of the world: to seek onself and the visible.[4] The Spirit of Jesus is to live not for oneself and not for the visible but for God and the things that are invisible.[5]

It is a very terrible and serious thought that one can carry on a busy life, free from manifest sin or unrighteousness, and yet remain in the friendship of the world and thereby in enmity against God.[6]

Where the care for the world—for what we eat and what we should drink, for what we possess or may still get into possession, for what we can have brought forth in the earth and made to increase—is the chief element in our life, there we are conformed to this world. It is a terrible and a very serious thought that one can maintain an appearance of a Christian life and think that one is trusting in Christ while yet living with the world for self and the visible.[7] For this reason the command comes to all Christians with great emphasis: Be conformed not to this world but to Jesus.

And how can I come to not be conformed to this world? Read our verse over again with consideration; we read there two things. Observe what goes before. It is those who have presented their bodies to God as a sacrifice on the altar who have it said to them, "Be not conformed to this world." Offer yourself to God—that is conformity to Jesus. Live every day as one that is offered to God, crucified in Christ to the world; then you will not be conformed to the world.[8]

---

[3]1 John 2:15, 16
[4]John 5:44
[5]2 Cor. 4:13; 5:7, 15
[6]James 4:4
[7]Matt. 6:32, 33
[8]Gal. 6:14

Observe also what follows: Be transformed by the renewing of your mind, that ye may prove what is the perfect will of God. There must be a continuous renewal of our mind. This takes place by the Holy Spirit when we let ourselves be led by Him. Then we learn to judge spiritually what is according to the will of God and what is according to the spirit of the world. A Christian who strives after the progressive renewal of his whole mind shall not be conformed to the world; the Spirit of God makes him conformed to Jesus.[9]

Believers, believe that Jesus has obtained for you the power to overcome the world, with its deep seductions to living for ourselves. Believe this: believe in Him as victor, and you also have the victory.[10]

Precious Lord, we have presented ourselves to you as living sacrifices. We have offered ourselves to God. We are not of the world even as you are not of the world. Lord, let our mind be enlightened by the renewing of the Holy Spirit that we may rightly see what the spirit of this world is. And let it be seen in us that we are not of this world but are conformed to Jesus. Amen.

1. *Worldly pleasures.* Is dancing sin? What harm is there in social drinking? May a Christian go to a Sunday football game? One has sometimes wished that there were in the Scriptures a distinct law to forbid such things. God has intentionally not given this. If there were such a law, it would make men only externally religious. God is concerned with the inner man—whether his inner disposition is worldly or heavenly. Learn Rom. 12:1, 2 by heart and ask the Spirit of God to make it living in you. The Christian who offers himself to God and becomes transformed by the renewing of the mind to prove the perfect will of God will learn whether he may dance or go to Sunday football games. The Christian

---

[9] 2 Cor. 6:14, 16; Eph. 5:17; Heb. 5:14
[10] John 16:33; 1 John 5:4, 5

must learn to see what the Spirit of God gives His children to see.

2. It is remarkable that the trinity of the god of this world, in John's Epistle, is seen as well in the temptation in Paradise and in that of the Lord Jesus.

Temptation	The lust of the flesh	The lust of the eyes	The vainglory of life
Adam and Eve	The woman saw that the tree was good for food.	And that it was a delight to the eyes.	And that the tree was to be desired to make one wise.
Jesus Christ	Command that those stones become bread.	The devil showeth him all the kingdoms of the world.	Cast thyself down.

3. Remember: it is only conformity to Jesus that will keep out conformity to the world. Let conformity to Jesus be the study, the endeavor of your soul.

CHAPTER 41

The Lord's Day

"And God blessed the seventh day, and sanctified it: because that in it he had rested from all his work which God created" (Gen. 2:3).

"Then the same day at evening, being the first day of the week . . . came Jesus and stood in the midst, and saith unto them, Peace be unto you" (John 20:19).

"I was in the Spirit on the Lord's day" (Rev. 1:10).

Man abides under the law of time. He must have time for what he would do or obtain. In a wonderful way God gives him time for communion with himself. One day in seven God separated for fellowship with himself.

The great object of God's gift of this day is said to be that it may serve as an expression that God desires to sanctify man.[1] Endeavor to understand well that word "holy." It is one of the most important words in the Bible.

God is the Holy One; God communicates His holiness by revealing himself to us. We know that the temple was holy, because God dwelt there. God had taken possession of it. So would God also sanctify man, take possession of him, fill him with himself, with His own life, His disposition, His holiness. For this reason God took possession of the seventh day, appropriating it to himself. He sanctified it. And He calls man also to sanctify it and to acknowledge it as the Lord's day, the day of the Lord's presence and special working. He that does this, that sanctifies this day, shall, as God has promised,

---

[1] Ex. 31:13, 17; Ezek. 20:12, 20

160

be sanctified by Him. (Read with attention Ex. 31:12–17, especially verse 13.)

God blessed the seventh day by sanctifying it. The blessing of God is the power of life, lodged by Him in anything whereby it has a result full of blessing. Grass, and cattle, and man He blessed with power to multiply.[2] And so He lodged in the seventh day a power to bless—that promise that everyone that sanctifies this day shall be sanctified and blessed by it. We must think of the Sabbath as a blessed day that certainly brings blessing. The blessing bound up with it is very great.[3]

There is still a third word that is used of the institution of the Sabbath: "God rested on the seventh day," and, as it stands in Exodus, "was refreshed" or gladdened. God would sanctify and bless us by introducing us into His rest. He would bring us to see that we are not to burden ourselves with our cares and weaknesses. We are to rest in Him, in His finished work, in His rest, which He takes because all is in order. This rest is not the outward cessation of employments; no, it is the rest of faith by which we cease from our works as God did from His because all is finished. Into this rest we enter by faith in the finished work of Jesus, in surrender to be sanctified by God.[4]

Because Jesus finished the second creation in His resurrection, and we by the power of His resurrection enter into life and rest, the seventh day is changed to the first day of the week. There is no specific statement on this point; under the New Testament, the Spirit takes the place of the law. The Spirit of the Lord led His disciples to the celebration of this day not only on which the Lord was raised but also on which, in all likelihood, the Spirit was poured out; not only on which the Lord manifested himself during the forty days but on which the Spirit also especially worked.[5]

---

[2]Gen. 1:22, 28; 22:17
[3]Isa. 56:4–7; 58:13, 14
[4]Heb. 4:3, 10
[5]John 20:1, 19, 26; Acts 1:8; 20:7; 1 Cor. 16:2; Rev. 1:10

The chief lessons that we have to learn about this day are the following:

The principal aim of the Sabbath is to make you holy as God is holy. God would have you holy. This is glory, this is blessedness, this is His blessing, this is His rest. God would have you holy, filled with himself and His holiness.[6]

In order to sanctify you, God must have you with Him in His presence and fellowship. You are to come away from all your struggling and working to rest with Him—to rest quietly, without exertion or anxiety, in the certainty that the Son has finished everything, that the Father cares for you in everything, that the Spirit will work everything in you. In the holy rest of a soul that is silent toward God, that remains silent before His presence to hear what God speaks to him, that depends upon God to achieve all, God can reveal himself.[7] It is thus that He sanctifies us.

We sanctify the day of rest first by withdrawal from all external business and detraction, but especially by employing it as God's day, belonging to the Lord, for what He destined it—fellowship with himself.

Take heed, on the other hand, that you do not use the day of rest only as a day for the public observance of divine worship. It is especially in private, personal communion that God can bless and sanctify you. In the church, the understanding is kept active and you have the ordinances of preaching, united prayer and praise to keep you occupied. But we do not always know whether the heart is really dealing with God, is taking delight in Him. This takes place in solitude. Oh, accustom yourself, then, to be alone with the Lord your God. Do not only speak to Him. Let Him speak to you; let your heart be the temple in whose holy silence His voice is heard. Rest in God; then will God say of your heart, "This is my rest; here will I dwell."[8]

New believer, do not miss the fullness of this blessed day

---

[6]Ex. 29:43, 45; Ezek. 37:27, 28; 1 Pet. 1:15, 16

[7]Ps. 62:2, 6; Hab. 2:20; Zech. 2:13; John 19:30

[8]Ps. 132:13, 14

of rest. Long for it. Thank God for it. Keep it very holy. And, above all, let it be a day of inner fellowship with your God, of a living communion with His love.

Holy God, I thank you for the holy day which you have given me as a token that you will sanctify me. Lord God, you sanctified this day by taking it for yourself. Sanctify me in like manner by taking me for yourself. Teach me to enter into your rest, so to find my rest in your love, that my whole soul shall be silent before you in order that you may make yourself and your love known to me. And let every Sabbath be to me a foretaste of the eternal rest with you. Amen.

1. The Sabbath was the first of all the means of grace, instituted even before the Fall. You cannot set too high a value upon it.

2. Observe how especially the Three-One God has revealed himself upon the day of rest. The Father rested on this day. The Son rose from the dead on it. The Spirit sanctified this day by His special workings. You may on this day expect His fellowship and powerful workings.

3. What is meant by the word "holy"? Of what is the day of rest an expression, according to Ex. 31:13? How did God sanctify the day of rest? How does He sanctify us?

4. There are difficulties in the way of the quiet celebration of the day of rest. Yet, one can lay aside that which is unnecessary and allow the Sabbath to have its full effect.

5. It is a matter of great importance to bring up children for the sanctification of the Sabbath day by setting a proper example for them of this day. Children should be engaged in a Sunday school and the church service. What they see in their parents' attitude will be followed.

6. There is no better day than the Lord's day for doing good to body and soul. Let the works of Satan on this day come to an end, and work for the lost and the ignorant be carried forward.

7. The principal point is this: the day of rest is the day of God's rest, of rest in and with God, and of fellowship with Him. It is God who will sanctify us. He does this by taking possession of us.

CHAPTER 42

Holy Baptism

"Go ye therefore, and teach all nations, baptizing them in the name of the Father, and of the Son, and of the Holy Ghost: teaching them to observe all things whatsoever I have commanded you" (Matt. 28:19).

"He that believeth and is baptized shall be saved" (Mark 16:16).

In these words of the institution of baptism, we find its meaning comprehended as in a summary. The word "teach" means to "make disciples of all the nations, baptizing them." The believing disciple, as he is baptized in the water, is also to be baptized or introduced into the name of the Three-One God.

By the name of the Father, the new birth and life as a child in the love of the Father are secured to him;[1] by the name of the Son, participation in the forgiveness of sins and the life that is in Christ;[2] by the name of the Holy Spirit, the indwelling and progressive renewal of the Spirit.[3] And every baptized believer must look upon baptism as his entrance into a covenant with the Three-One God and as a pledge that the Father, the Son, and the Spirit will in the course of time do for him all that they have promised. It requires a lifelong study to know and enjoy all the blessing that is presented in baptism.

---

[1]Gal. 3:26, 27; 4:6, 7
[2]Col. 2:12
[3]Titus 3:5, 6

166

In other passages of scripture this blessing is again set forth separately; thus we find bound up with it the new birth required to make a child of God. "Except a man be born of water and the Spirit, he cannot enter into the kingdom of God." The baptized disciple has in God a Father, and he has to live as a child in the love of this Father.[4]

Then, again, baptism is brought more directly into connection with the redemption that is in Christ. Consequently, the first and simplest representation of it is the forgiveness or washing away of sins. Forgiveness is always the gateway or entrance into all blessing; hence baptism is also the sacrament of the beginning of the Christian life, but of a beginning that is maintained through the whole life.

It is on this account that in Romans 6 baptism is represented as the secret of sanctification, the entrance into a life in union with Jesus. "Or are ye ignorant that all we who were baptized into Christ Jesus were baptized into his death?" And then follows in verses 4 through 11 the more precise explanation of what it is to be baptized into the death of Jesus and to arise out of this with Him for a new life in Him. This is elsewhere very powerfully comprehended in these words: "As many of you as were baptized into Christ did put on Christ." This alone is the right life of a baptized disciple: he has put on Christ.[5] The believing confessor is baptized into the death of Christ in order to live and walk clothed with the new life of Christ.

And there are other passages where there is connected with baptism the promise of the Spirit, not only as the Spirit of regeneration but as the gift bestowed from heaven upon believers for indwelling and sealing, for progressive renewal. "He saved us through the washing of regeneration and renewing of the Holy Ghost, which he poured out upon us richly." Renewal is here the activity of the Spirit whereby the new life that is planted in the new birth penetrates our

[4]John 3:3, 5
[5]Rom. 6:3, 4; Gal. 3:27; Col. 2:12

whole being, so that all our thinking and doing is sanctified by Him.[6]

And all this rich blessing which lies in baptism is received by faith. "He that believeth, and is baptized, shall be saved." Baptism was not only a confession on man's part of the faith that he already had but equally on God's part a seal for the confirmation of faith, a covenant token in which the whole treasury of grace lay open, to be enjoyed throughout life.

As often as a baptized believer sees a baptism administered, or reflects upon it, it is to be to him an encouragement to press on to an ever-growing faith in the full life of salvation that God desires to work in him. The Holy Spirit is given to appropriate within us all the love of the Father and all the grace of the Son. The believing candidate for baptism who is baptized into the death of Christ has put on Christ. The Holy Spirit is in him to give him all this as his daily experience.[7]

Lord God, make your holy baptism always operative in my soul as the experience that I am baptized into the death of Christ. And let your people everywhere understand by your Spirit what rich blessing lies open to them in baptism. Amen.

---

[6]Rom. 12:2; Eph. 4:23; Titus 3:5, 6
[7]John 16:13, 14; Eph. 4:14, 15; Col. 2:6

CHAPTER 43

The Lord's Supper

"The cup of blessing which we bless, is it not the com-munion of the blood of Christ? The bread which we break, is it not the communion of the body of Christ?" (1 Cor. 10:16).

"He that eateth my flesh, and drinketh my blood, dwelleth in me, and I in him. . . . He that eateth me, even he shall live by me" (John 6:56, 57).

All living things have need of food; it is sustained by nourishment which it takes in from outside itself. The heavenly life must have heavenly food; nothing less than Jesus himself is the bread of life: "He that eateth me shall live by me."[1]

This heavenly food, Jesus, is brought near to us in two of the means of grace—the Word and the Lord's Supper. The Word comes to present Jesus to us from the side of the intellectual life—by our thoughts. The Lord's Supper comes in like manner to present Jesus to us from the side of the emotional life—by the physical senses. Man has both a spirit and body. Redemption begins with the spirit, but it would also penetrate to the body.[2] Redemption is not complete until this mortal body also shall share in glory.

The Supper is the pledge that the Lord will also change our earthly body and make it like His own glorified body by the working whereby He subdues all things to himself. It is not simply because all that is physical is more clear and

---

[1]Ps. 13:3; Matt. 4:4; John 6:51
[2]Rom. 8:23; 1 Cor. 6:13, 15, 19, 20; Phil. 3:21

intelligible for us that the Lord gives himself in the bread of the Supper. No, by the body Scripture often means the whole man.

In the Supper, Christ would take possession of the whole man—body and soul—to renew and sanctify it by the power of His holy body and blood. Even His body is communicated by the Holy Spirit. Even our body is fed with His holy body and renewed by the working of the Holy Spirit.[3]

This feeding with the body of Christ has two aspects: on the side of the Lord, by the Spirit; on our side, by faith.

On the side of the Lord by the Spirit—the Spirit communicates to us the power of the glorified body whereby even our bodies, according to Scripture, become members of His body.[4] The Spirit causes us to drink of the life-power of His blood, so that the blood becomes the life and joy of our soul. The bread is a participation in the body; the cup is a participation in the blood.

And this takes place on our side by faith—a faith that, above what can be seen or understood, depends upon the wonder-working power of the Holy Spirit to unite us really, alike in soul and body, with our Lord by communicating Him inwardly to us.[5]

This is how the Heidelberg Catechism defines it:

"What is it to eat the glorified body of Christ and to drink His shed blood?

"It is not only to receive with a believing heart the whole suffering and dying of Christ, and thereby to obtain forgiveness of sins and eternal life, but also therewith, by the Holy Spirit, who dwells alike in Christ and in us, to be so united more and more with His blessed body that we, although He is in heaven and we are upon earth, are nevertheless flesh of His flesh and bone of His bone, and so live and are governed eternally by one Spirit, as members of our body by a soul."*

---

[3]Matt. 26:26; John 6:54, 55; Rom. 8:11, 13

[4]1 Cor. 6:15, 17; 12:13; Eph. 5:23, 30

[5]Luke 1:37; 1 Cor. 2:9, 12

*Der Heidelbergische Catechismus, Section 28, 5:76

This deeply inward union with Jesus, even with His body and blood, is the great aim of the Lord's Supper. All that it teaches and gives us—the forgiveness of sin, the remembrance of Jesus, the confirmation of the divine covenant, union with one another, the announcement of the Lord's death till He comes—must lead to this: complete oneness with Jesus through the Spirit.[6] "He that eateth my flesh and drinketh my blood dwelleth in me, and I in him. He that eateth me, even he shall live by me."

It is readily understood that the blessing of the Supper depends very much on preparation within the inner chamber, on the hunger and thirst with which one longs for the living God.[7] Do not imagine, however, that the Supper is nothing but a symbolic expression of what we already have by faith in the Word. No, it is an actual spiritual communication from the exalted Lord in heaven of the powers of His life; yet this is only according to the measure of desire and faith. Prepare for the Lord's Supper, therefore, with very earnest separation and prayer. And then expect that the Lord will, with His heavenly power, renew your life in a way to you incomprehensible, yet sure.

Blessed Lord, who instituted the Supper in order to communicate yourself to your redeemed as their food and their power of life, oh, teach us to use the Supper. Teach us at every opportunity to eat and to drink with great hunger and thirst for yourself and for full union with you, believing that the Holy Spirit feeds us with your body and gives us to drink of your blood. Amen.

1. In connection with the Supper, let us be on our guard against the idea of it being just another church service or a service where emotions are played upon. Preaching and testimonies may make an edifying impression, while there is little power or blessing.

---

[6]Matt. 26:28; Luke 22:19; John 6:56; 15:4; 1 Cor. 10:17; 11:26; Rev. 3:20
[7]Job 11:13; Isa. 55:1, 3; Matt. 5:6; Luke 1:53; 1 Cor. 11:28

2. For a meal, the first requisite is hunger. A strong hunger and thirst for God is indispensable.

3. In the Supper, Jesus desires to give himself to us, and would have us give ourselves to Him. These are great and holy things.

4. The lessons of the Supper are many. It is a feast of remembrance, a feast of reconciliation, a covenant feast, a love feast, a feast of hope. But all these separate thoughts are only subordinate parts of the principal element: the living Jesus would give himself to us in the most inward union. The Son of God would descend into our innermost parts; He would come in to celebrate the Supper with us. "He that eateth my flesh and drinketh my blood, dwelleth in me, and I in him."

5. And then union with Jesus is union with His people in love and sympathy.

6. The preparatory address is not itself the preparation; it is only a help to the private preparation which one must have in communion with Jesus.

7. To hold festival with God at His table is something of unspeakable importance. Do not suppose that because you are a Christian it is easy for you to go and sit down. No, separate yourself in solitude with Jesus that He may speak to you and say how you are to prepare your heart to eat with Him—yes, with himself.

CHAPTER 44

Obedience

"Now therefore, if ye will obey my voice indeed . . . ye shall be a peculiar treasure unto me above all people" (Ex. 19:5).

"The Lord shall greatly bless thee . . . if thou carefully hearken unto the voice of the Lord thy God" (Deut. 15:4, 5).

"By faith Abraham . . . obeyed" (Heb. 11:8).

"Though he were a Son, yet learned he obedience by the things which he suffered; and being made perfect, he became the author of eternal salvation unto all them that obey him" (Heb. 5:8, 9).

Obedience is one of the most important words in the life of the believer. It was through disobedience that man lost the favor and the life of God. It is only in the way of obedience that that favor and that life can again be enjoyed.[1] God cannot possibly take pleasure in those who are not obedient, nor can He bestow His blessing upon them. "If ye will obey my voice indeed . . . if thou carefully hearken unto the voice of the Lord thy God." These are the eternal principles specifying how man can enjoy God's favor and blessing.

We see this in the Lord Jesus. He says, "If ye keep my commandments, ye shall abide in my love; even as I have kept my Father's commandments, and abide in his love." He was in the love of the Father but could abide there only by obedience. And He says that this is equally for us the one way to abide in His love: we must keep His commandments. He came to open the way back to God for us; this way was

---

[1] Rom. 5:19; 6:16; 1 Pet. 1:2, 14, 22

the way of obedience, and only he that through faith in Jesus walks in this way shall come to God.[2]

This connection between the obedience of Jesus and our own is expressed in Hebrews 5: He "learned obedience ... and became the author of eternal salvation unto all them that obey him." This is the bond of unity between Jesus and His people, the point of conformity and inward unanimity. He was obedient to the Father; they, on the other hand, are obedient to Him. He and they are both obedient. His obedience not only atones for but drives out their disobedience. He and they bear one expression—obedience to God.[3]

This obedience is a characteristic of the life of faith. It is called the obedience of faith.[4] There is nothing in earthly things that so spurs men to work as faith—the belief that there is advantage or joy to be found is the secret of all work. "By faith Abraham, when he was called, obeyed"; according to what I believe shall my works be. The faith that Jesus made me free from the power of sin for obedience and has equipped me for a life of obedience has a mighty power to make me obedient. Faith in the overflowing blessing which the Father gives to it, faith in the promises of love and indwelling of God, of the fullness of the Spirit which comes by this channel, strengthens for obedience.[5]

The power of this faith, as also of obedience, lies especially in fellowship with the living God himself. There is but one Hebrew word for "*obeying* voice" and "*hearing* voice": to hear correctly prepares to obey. It is when I learn the will of God not in the words of a man or a book but from God himself—when I hear the *voice* of God—that I shall surely believe what is promised and do what is commanded.

The Holy Spirit is the voice of God; when we hear the living voice speak, obedience becomes easy.[6] Oh, let us then wait in silence upon God and set our soul open before Him

---

[2]Gen. 22:17, 18; 26:4, 5; 1 Sam. 15:22; John 15:10

[3]Rom. 6:17; 2 Cor. 10:5; Phil. 2:8

[4]Acts 6:7; Rom. 1:5; 16:26

[5]Deut. 28:1; Isa. 63:7–9; John 14:11, 15, 23; Acts 5:32

[6]Gen. 12:1, 4; 31:13, 16; Matt. 14:28; Luke 5:5; John 10:4, 27

174

that He may speak by His Spirit. When in our Bible reading and praying we learn to wait more upon God so that we can say, "My God has spoken this to me, has given me this promise, has commanded this," then shall we also obey. "To listen to the voice" earnestly, diligently, is the sure way to obedience.

With a servant, a warrior, a child, a subject, obedience is indispensable, the first expression of integrity. And shall God, the living, glorious God, find no obedience with us?[7] No. Let cheerful, punctual, precise obedience from the beginning be the expression of the genuineness of our fellowship with the Son whose obedience is our life.

O Father, who has made us your children in Christ, you make us in Him obedient children as He was obedient. Let the Holy Spirit make the obedience of Jesus so glorious and powerful in us that obedience shall be the highest joy of our life. Teach us in everything only to seek to know what you desire and then to do it. Amen.

For a life of obedience the following things are required:

1. *Decisive surrender.* I must no longer have to ask in every single case, "Shall I or shall I not, must I, can I, be obedient?" No, it must be such an unquestionable thing that I shall know of nothing else than to be obedient. He that has this character and thinks of obedience as a thing that stands firm shall find it easy—yes, shall literally taste in it great joy.

2. *The knowledge of God's will* through the Spirit. Do not imagine that because you know the Bible in some sort, you know the will of God. The knowledge of God's will is something spiritual; let the Holy Spirit make known to you the knowledge of God's will.

3. *The doing of all that we know to be right.* All doing teaches men; all doing of what is right teaches men obedience. Actually do all that the Word, or conscience, or the

---

[7]Mal. 1:6; Matt. 7:21

Spirit tells you is correct. It helps to form doing into a holy habit, and is an exercise leading to more power and more knowledge. Do what is right out of obedience to God and you shall be blessed.

4. *Faith in the power of Christ.* You have the power to obey; be sure of this. Although you may not feel it, you have it in Christ your Lord by faith.

5. *The glad assurance of the blessing of obedience.* It unites us with our God; it wins His good pleasure and love; it strengthens our life; it brings the blessedness of heaven into our heart.

CHAPTER 45

The Will of God

"Thy will be done in earth, as it is in heaven" (Matt. 6:10).

The glory of heaven, where the Father dwells, is that His will is done there. He who would taste the blessedness of heaven must know the Father who is there and do His will as it is done in heaven.[1]

"Heaven is an unending holy kingdom, of which the throne of God is the central point. Around this throne there are innumerable multitudes of pure, free beings, all ordered under powers and dominions. An indescribably rich and many-sided activity fills their life. All the highest and noblest that keeps man occupied is but a faint shadow of what finds place in this invisible world. All these beings possess their own free personal will. The will, however, has in self-conscious freedom, by its own choice, become one with the holy will of the holy Father, so that in the midst of a diversity that flashes out in a million forms, only one will is accomplished—the will of God. All the rich, blessed movement of the inhabitants of heaven has its origin and its aim in the will of God."

And why is it, then, that His children on earth do not regard this will as their highest joy? Why is it that the petition "Thy will be done as in heaven" is for the most part coupled with thoughts of the severe, hard will of God, of the impossibility of our always rejoicing in God's will? The reason is this: we do not take pains to know the will of God in

---

[1]Dan. 4:35

its glory and beauty, as the expression of God's love, as the source of power and joy, as the expression of the perfection of God. We think of God's will only in the law that He gave and that we cannot keep, or in the trials in which this will appears in conflict with our own. Oh, let us no longer do this, but take pains to understand that *in* the will of God all His love and blessedness are comprehended and can be received by us.[2]

Hear what the Word says about the will of God and the glorious things that are destined for us in this will.

"This is the will of my Father, that every one that beholdeth the Son and believeth on him should have eternal life." The will of God is the rescue of sinners by faith in Christ. He that surrenders himself to this glorious will to seek souls shall have the assurance that God will bless his work to others; for he carries out God's will even as Jesus did.[3]

"It is not the will of your Father which is in heaven that one of these little ones should perish." The will of God is the maintenance, the strengthening, the keeping of the weakest of His children. What courage shall he have who unites himself with this will.[4]

"This is the will of God, even your sanctification." With His whole heart, with all the power of His will, God is willing to make us holy. If we but open our heart to believe that it is not the law but the will of God—something that He certainly gives and does where we permit Him—then shall we rejoice over our sanctification as stable and sure.[5]

"In everything give thanks: for this is the will of God in Christ Jesus concerning you." A joyful, thankful life is what God has destined for us, is what He will work in us: what He desires, that He certainly does in those who do not withstand Him but receive and allow His will to work in them.[6]

What we require, then, is to surrender our spirit to be

---

[2]Gal. 1:4; Eph. 1:5, 9, 11; Heb. 10:10
[3]John 4:34; 5:20; 6:38, 40
[4]Matt. 18:14
[5]1 Thess. 4:3; 5:23, 24
[6]1 Thess. 5:18

filled with the thought that what God would have He will certainly bring to pass when we do not resist Him. And if we further consider how glorious, and good, and perfect the will of God is, shall we not then yield ourselves with the whole heart that this will may bring itself to accomplishment in us?[7]

To this end, let us believe that the will of God is His love. Let us see what blessings in the Word are connected with the doing of this will.[8] Let us think of the glory of heaven as consisting in doing God's will, and make the choice that our life on earth shall be the same. Let us with prayer and meditation allow ourselves to be led of the Spirit to understand this will.[9]

When we have thus learned to know the will of God on its glorious heavenly side in the Word and have done it, it will not be difficult for us also to bear this will where it appears to be contrary to our nature. We shall be so filled with the adoration of God and His will that we shall resolve to see, and approve, and love this will in everything. And it will be the most glorious thought of our life that there is to be nothing, nothing, in which the will of God must not be known and honored.[10]

O my Father, this was the glory of Jesus: that He did not His own will but the will of His Father. This His glory I desire to have as mine. Father, open my eyes and my heart to know the perfection, the glory, of your will and the glory of a life in this will. Teach me to understand your will, then willingly and cheerfully to execute it; and where I have to bear it, to do this also with loving adoration. Amen.

1. To do the will of God from the heart in times of prosperity is the only way to bear this will from the heart in times of suffering.

---

[7]Rom. 12:2
[8]Matt. 7:21; 12:50; John 7:17; 9:31; Eph. 5:17; 6:6; 1 John 2:17
[9]Rom. 12:2; Col. 1:9; 4:12; Heb. 10:36; 13:21
[10]Matt. 26:39; Heb. 10:7, 9

2. To do the will of God, I must know it spiritually. The light and the power of the Spirit go together: what He teaches to see as God's will, He certainly teaches all to do. Meditate much on Rom. 12:2, and pray earnestly to see God's will correctly.

3. Learn to adore the will of God even in the worst thing that man does to you. It is not the will of God that man should do what is sinful; but when man does sin, it is the will of God that His child should be proved thereby. Say then always in the least as well as the greatest trials: "It is the will of God that I am in this difficulty." This brings the soul to rest and silence and teaches it to honor God in the trial.

4. When God gave man a will, He gave him a power whereby he could accept or reject the will of God. New believer, open your will to receive the will of God with its full power, and to be filled with it. This is heavenly glory and blessedness: to be conscious every day that "my will is in harmony with God's will; God's will lives in me." It is the will of God to work this in you.

CHAPTER 46

Self-denial

"Then said Jesus unto his disciples, If any man will come after me, let him deny himself, and take up his cross and follow me" (Matt. 16:24).

Self-denial was an exercise of which the Lord Jesus often spoke. He mentioned it several times as an indispensable expression of every true disciple. He connects it with cross-bearing and losing life.[1] Our old life was so sinful that it had to be crucified with Christ. It must therefore be denied and mortified in order that the new life, the life of God, may have free dominion over us.[2] Let the new believer choose from the very beginning to deny himself wholly, in accordance with the word of his Lord. At the outset it seems severe, but he will find that it is the source of inconceivable blessing.

Let self-denial reach our carnal understanding. It was when Peter had spoken according to the thought of the natural understanding that the Lord had to say to him, "Thou mindest not the things of God, but the things of men." You must deny yourself and your own thoughts. We must be careful that the activity of our understanding of the Word and prayer, in endeavoring to know the knowledge of God's will, does not deceive us with a perception of God that is not in spirit and in truth. Deny your carnal understanding; bring it to silence. In holy silence give place to the Holy Spirit; let

---

[1]Matt. 10:38, 39; Luke 9:23; 14:27; John 12:24, 25
[2]Rom. 6:6, 8:13; Gal. 2:20; 5:24; 6:14; Col. 3:5

the voice of God be heard in your heart.[3]

Deny also your own will, with all it lusts and desires. Let it be once for all unquestionable that the will of God in everything is your choice, and that therefore every desire that does not fall in with this will must be put to death. Believe that in the will of God there is heavenly blessedness and that therefore self-denial appears severe only at the outset; but when you exercise yourself heartily in it, His will becomes a great joy. Let the body with all its life abide under the law of self-denial.[4]

Deny also your own honor. Do not seek it, but seek the honor of God. This brings such a rest into the soul. "How can ye believe," says Jesus, "which receive glory one of another?" Although your honor be hurt or reviled, commit it to God to watch over it. Be content to be little, to be nothing. "Blessed are the poor in spirit, for theirs is the kingdom."[5]

Deny, in like manner, your own power. Understand the deep conviction that it is those who are weak, those who are nothing, that God can use. Beware of your own endeavors in the service of God, however sincere they may be. Although you feel as if you had power, say before God that you have it not, that your power is nothing; continuous denial of your own power is the way to enjoy the power of God. It is in the heart which dies to its own power that the Holy Spirit comes to dwell and bring the power of God.[6]

Deny especially your own interests. Live not to please yourself but your neighbor. He who seeks his own life shall lose it; he who would live for himself shall not find life. But he who would really imitate Jesus, to share in His joy, let him give his life as He did, let him sacrifice his own interests.[7]

At conversion you had to make a choice as to which you should obey—your own self or Christ. You then said, "Not I,

---

[3]Matt. 16:23; 1 Cor. 1:17, 27; 2:6; Col. 2:18
[4]Matt. 26:39; Rom. 6:13; 1 Cor. 9:25, 27
[5]Matt. 5:3; John 5:44; 7:18; 8:50; 1 Thess. 2:6
[6]2 Cor. 3:5; 12:9
[7]Rom. 15:1, 3; 1 Cor. 10:23, 24; Eph. 5:2

but Christ." Now you are to confirm this choice every day. The more you do so, the more joyful and blessed will it be for you to renounce the sinful self, to cast aside unholy self-working, and allow Jesus to be all. The way of self-denial is a way of deep heavenly blessedness.

There are very many Christians who do not live like this. They would have Jesus to make them free from punishment but not to liberate them from themselves, from their own will. But the invitation to discipleship still always rings: "If any man would come after me, let him deny himself, and take up his cross and follow me."

The reason as well as the power for self-denial is found in the little word *me*. "If any man would come after *me*, let him deny *himself . . .* and follow *me*." The old life is in ourselves; the new life is in Jesus. The new life cannot rule without driving out the old. Where one's own self had everything to say, it must be nothing. On this account there must be the daily denial of oneself and imitation of Jesus. He, with His teaching, His will, His honor, His interests, must fill the heart. But he that has and knows Him willingly denies himself; Christ is so precious to him that he sacrifices everything, even himself, to win Him.[8]

This is the true life of faith. I live not according to what nature sees or thinks to be acceptable but according to what Jesus says and would have. Every day and every hour I confirm the wonderful bargain: "Not I, but Christ"—I nothing, Christ everything. "Ye died," and no longer have power, or will, or honor: "Your life is hid with Christ in God." Christ's power and will alone prevail. O soul, cheerfully deny that sinful wretched self in order that the glorious Christ may dwell in you.

Precious Savior, teach me what self-denial is. Teach me so to distrust my heart that in nothing shall I yield to its fancy. Teach me so to know you that it shall be impossible for me to

---

[8]Gal. 2:20; Phil. 3:7, 8

do anything else than to offer up myself to possess you and your life. Amen.

1. Of the denial of the natural understanding Tersteegen says: "God and His truth are never known aright, save by such a one as, by the dying of his carnal nature, his inclinations, passions, and will, is made very earnest and silent; and by the abandonment of the manifold deliberations of the understanding has become very simple and childlike. We must give our heart and our will entirely to God, forsaking our own will in all things, releasing ourselves especially from the manifold imaginations and activities of the understanding, even in spiritual things, that it may collect itself silently in the heart and dwell as in the heart with God. Not in the head but in the heart does the true understanding display itself in acquiring the knowledge of God. In the head are the barren ideas of truth; in the heart is found the living truth itself, the anointing that teaches us all things. In the heart is found the living fountain of light. Anyone that lives in a heart entertained with God will often with a glance of the eye discern more truth than another with the greatest exertion."

2. Read the above passage with care; you will find in it the reason why we have several times said that when you read or pray, you must at every opportunity keep quiet for a little and set yourself in entire silence before God. This is necessary to bring the activity of the natural understanding to silence and to set the heart open before God that He may speak there. In the heart is the temple where worship in spirit and truth takes place. Distrust and deny your understanding in spiritual things. The natural understanding is in the head; the spiritual understanding is in the heart, the temple of God. Oh, preserve in the temple of God a holy silence before His countenance; then He will speak.

3. "The peculiar mark of Christian self-denial is inward cheerfulness and joy in the midst of privation. The Word of God makes unceasing joy of duty. This gladsome disposition, which, hailing from eternity, has all change and vicissitude

184

under foot, will hold its ground not only in times of severe suffering but also in the self-denial of every day and hour that is inseparable from the Christ life."

4. What am I to deny? Deny yourself. How shall I know where and when to deny myself? Do so always and in everything. And if you do not rightly understand the answer, know that no one can give you the right explanation of it but Jesus himself. To imitate Him, to be taught of Him, is the only way to self-denial. *Only when Jesus comes in does self go out.*

CHAPTER 47

Discretion

"When wisdom entereth into thine heart, and knowledge is pleasant unto thy soul; discretion shall preserve thee; understanding shall keep thee" (Prov. 2:10, 11).

"My son . . . keep sound wisdom and discretion: so shall they be life unto thy soul" (Prov. 3:21, 22).

"Ye ought to be quiet, and to do nothing rash" (Acts 19:36).

Indiscretion is not only the sin of the unconverted. Among the people of God, it is often the cause of much evil and misery. We read of Moses: "They angered him also at the waters of Meribah, so that it went ill with Moses for their sakes: because they were rebellious against his spirit, and he spake unadvisedly with his lips." We read also of Uzzah's touching the ark: "And God smote him there for his error [marg., rashness]."[1]

What discretion is, and why it is so necessary, may be easily explained. When an army marches into the province of an enemy, its safety depends on the guards which are set, which are to be always on the watch to know and to give warning when the enemy approaches. Advance guards are sent out that the territory and power of the enemy may be known. This prudence, which looks out beforehand and looks around, is indispensable.

The Christian lives in the land of the enemy. All that surrounds him may become a snare or an occasion of sin. Therefore his whole walk is to be carried out in holy reserve

---

[1]2 Sam. 6:7; Ps.106:33; Prov. 12:18

and watchfulness in order that he may do nothing indiscreet. He watches and prays that he may not enter into temptation.[2] Prudence keeps guard over him.[3]

Discretion keeps watch over the lips. Oh, what loss many a child of God suffers by the thought that if he only speaks nothing wrong, he may speak what he wants. He does not know that through much speaking the soul becomes ensnared in the distractions of the world, because in the multitude of words there is not wanting transgression. Discretion endeavors not to speak except for the glory of God and blessing to neighbors.[4]

Discretion keeps guard also over the ear. Through the gate of the ear comes all the news of the world, all the indiscreet speech of others, which can infect me. Eagerness for news is very hurtful for the soul. Corinth was much more godless than Athens; but in this last place, where they "spent their time in nothing else but either to tell or to hear some new thing," very few were converted. Take heed, says Jesus, what you hear.[5]

On this account, discretion keeps watch over the society in which the Christian mingles. "He that separateth himself seeketh his own desire." The child of God has not the freedom to yield himself to the society of the world as often and as long as he would. He must know the will of his Father.[6]

Discretion keeps watch over all lawful occupations and possessions. It knows how gradually and stealthily the love of money, worldly mindedness, the secret power of the flesh, obtains the upper hand, and that it can never free itself from this temptation.[7]

And, above all, it keeps watch over the heart, because there are the issues of life, there is the fountain out of which everything springs. Remembering the word, "He that trust-

---

[2]Matt. 26:41; Luke 21:36; Eph. 6:18; 1 Pet. 4:7; 5:8

[3]1 Sam. 18:14; Matt. 10:16; Luke 1:17; 16:8; Eph. 5:15

[4]Ps. 39:2; 141:3; Prov. 10:19; Eccles. 5:1, 2

[5]Prov. 2:2; 18:15; Mark 4:24; Acts 17:21

[6]Ps. 1:1; Prov. 18:1; 2 Cor. 6:14; 2 Thess. 3:14; 2 John 10, 11

[7]Matt. 13:22; Luke 21:34; 1 Tim. 6:9, 17

eth in his own heart is a fool," it walks in deep humility and works out salvation with fear and trembling.[8]

And how does the soul have the power to be watchful, on its guard against the thousand dangers that surround it on all sides? Is it not fatiguing, exhausting, harassing to have to watch always and never to be at rest in the certainty that there is no danger? No, absolutely not. Discretion brings the highest restfulness. It has its security and strength in its heavenly Keeper, who slumbers not nor sleeps. In confidence in Him, under the inspiration of His Spirit, discretion does its work. The Christian walks as one that is wise; the dignity of holy discretion adorns him in all his actions. The rest of faith—the faith that Jesus watches and guards—binds to Him in love, and holy discretion springs as of its own accord from a love that would not grieve or abandon Him, from a faith that has its strength for everything in Him.

O Lord my God, guard me that I may not be of the indiscreet in heart. Let the discretion of the righteous always characterize me in order that in everything I may be kept from giving offense. Amen.

1. To one who took great care to have his horse and cart in thoroughly good order, it was once said, "Come, it is not necessary to be always taking so many pains with this." His answer was, "I have always found my prudence paid." How many believers have need of this lesson. How many a new believer may well pray for this—that his conversion may be, according to God's Word, "to the prudence of the righteous."

2. Discretion has its *root* in self-knowledge. The deeper my knowledge of my inability and the selfishness of my heart, the greater is the need of watchfulness. It is thus our element of true self-denial.

3. Discretion has its *power* in faith. The Lord is our keeper, and He does His keeping through the Spirit keeping us in mind. It is from Him that our discretion comes.

---

[8]Prov. 3:21, 23; 4:23; 28:18; Jer. 31:33

4. Its activity is not limited to ourselves; it reaches out especially to our neighbor, in giving him no offense and in laying no stumbling block in his way (Rom. 14:13; 1 Cor. 8:9; 10:32; Phil. 1:10).

5. It finds great delight in silence, so as to commit its way to the Lord with composure and deliberation. It esteems highly the word of the town clerk of Ephesus: "Ye ought to be quiet, and do nothing rash."

6. In great generals and their victories we see that discretion is not timidity; it is consistent with the highest courage and the most joyful certainty of victory. Discretion watches against rashness but enhances the courage of faith.

CHAPTER 48

Money

"Money answereth all things" (Eccles. 10:19).
"I had wholly dedicated the silver unto the Lord from my hand" (Judg. 17:3).
"Thou oughtest therefore to have put my money to the exchangers, and then at my coming I should have received back mine own with usury" (Matt. 25:27).

It is in his dealing with the world and its possessions that the Christian finds one of the opportunities in which he is to manifest his self-denial and the spirit of discretion.[1] Since it is in money that all value or property on earth still finds its expression, so it is especially in his dealing with money that he can show whether he is free from worldliness. In order to understand this, we must consider what is said about money.

What is money the expression of? It is the expression of the work by which a man earns it; of his industry, and zeal, and ability in that work; of his personal success and the provision of God upon him. It is also the token of all that I can do with money; the expression of the work that others would do for me, of the power that I thereby have to accomplish what I desire, of the influence which I exercise on those that are dependent upon me for my money; a token of all the possessions or enjoyments that are to be obtained by money; a token of all upon earth that can make life desirable—yes, an expression of life itself, which without the purchase of indispensable food cannot be supported.

---

[1]John 17:15, 16; 1 Cor. 7:31

Of earthly things, money is thus, one of the most desirable and fruitful. No wonder that it is thus esteemed by all.

What is the danger of money? What is the sin that is done with it, that the Bible and experience warn us to be prudent about? There is the anxiousness that does not know if there will be enough money.[2] There is the coveteousness that longs too much for it.[3] There is the dishonesty that without gross deception or theft does not give to a neighbor what belongs to him.[4] There is the lovelessness that would draw everything to oneself and does not keep another.[5] There is love of money which seeks after riches and lands in greediness.[6] There is robbery of God and the poor in withholding the share that belongs to them.[7]

What is the blessing of money? If the danger of sin is so great, would it not be better if there were no money? Is it not better to be without money? No, even for the spiritual life money may be a great blessing: as an exercise in industry and activity,[8] in care and economy; as an expression of God's blessing upon our work;[9] as an opportunity for showing that we can possess and lay it out for God without withholding it or cleaving to it, that by means of it we can manifest our generosity to the poor and our overflowing love for God's cause;[10] as a means of glorifying God by our beneficence, and of spreading among men the gold of heavenly blessing;[11] as a thing that, according to the assurance of Jesus, we can exhange for a treasure in heaven.[12]

And what is the way to be freed from the danger and to arrive at the blessing of money?

---

[2] Matt. 6:31
[3] 1 John 2:15, 16
[4] James 5:4
[5] Luke 16:19, 25
[6] 1 Tim. 6:9, 10, 17
[7] Prov. 3:27, 28; Mal. 3:8
[8] Eccles. 5:18, 19
[9] Prov. 10:4, 22
[10] 2 Cor. 8:14, 15
[11] 2 Cor. 9:12, 13
[12] Matt. 19:21; Luke 12:33

Let God be Lord over your money. Receive all your money with thanksgiving, as coming from God in answer to prayer, "Give us this day our daily bread."[13]

Lay it all down before God as belonging to Him. Say with David, "All things come of thee, and of thine own have we given thee."[14]

Let your dealing with your money be a part of your spiritual life. Receive, and possess, and give out your money as one who has been bought at a high price, redeemed not with silver and gold but with the precious blood.[15]

Make what the Word of God says of money and of worldly goods, a special study. The Word of the Father alone teaches how the child of the Father is to use the blessing of money.

Reflect much on the fact that it is not given to you for yourself alone but for you and your brethren together. The blessing of money is to do good to others and make them rejoice.[16]

Remember especially that it can be given to the Father and the service of His kingdom for the upbuilding of His spiritual temple, for the extension of His rule. Every time of spiritual blessing mentioned in Scripture was a time of cheerful giving to God's cause. Even the outpouring of the Holy Spirit made itself known in the giving of money for the Lord.[17]

Believer, understand it: all the deepest deliberations of the heart and its most spiritual activities will manifest themselves in the way in which we deal with our money. Love to God, love to neighbor, victory over the world by faith, the hope of everlasting treasure, faithfulness as steward, joy in God's service, cheerful self-denial, holy discretion, the glorious freedom of the children of God—all can be seen in the use of money. Money can be the means of the most glorious fellowship with God and the full enjoyment of the blessed-

---

[13]1 Chron. 29:14
[14]1 Chron. 29:12, 14
[15]Luke 19:8; 1 Pet. 1:18, 19
[16]Acts 20:35
[17]Ex. 36:5; 1 Chron. 29:6, 9; Acts 2:45; 4:34

ness of being able to honor and serve Him.

Lord God, cause me to discern in what close connection my money stands with my spiritual life. Let the Holy Spirit lead and sanctify me so that all my earning and receiving, my keeping and dispensing of money may always be well pleasing to you and a blessing to my soul. Amen.

1. John Wesley always said that there were three rules about the use of money which he gave to men in business and by which he was sure that they would experience benefit.
   a. Make as much money as you can. Be industrious and diligent.
   b. Save as much money as you can. Be no spendthrift; live frugally and prudently.
   c. Give away as much money as you can. That is the divine destination of money that makes it an everlasting blessing for yourselves and others.

2. Acquaint yourself with the magnificent prayer of David in 1 Chronicles 29. Receive it into your soul; it teaches us the blessedness and the glorification of God that spring from cheerful giving.

CHAPTER 49

The Freedom of the Christian

"Being then made free from sin, ye became the servants of righteousness. . . . Being made free from sin . . . ye have your fruit unto holiness" (Rom. 6:18, 22).

"But now we are delivered from the law" (Rom. 7:6).

"The law of the Spirit of life in Christ Jesus hath made me free from the law of sin and death" (Rom. 8:2).

Freedom is counted in Scripture as one of the greatest privileges of the child of God. There is nothing in history for which nations have made greater sacrifices than for freedom. Slavery is the lowest condition into which man can sink, for in it he can no longer arrange his own life. Freedom is the deepest need of his nature.

Freedom is the condition in which anything can develop itself according to the law of its nature—that is, according to its disposition. Without freedom nothing can attain its destiny or become what it ought to be. This is true of both animal and man, of the physical and the spiritual. It was for this reason that God chose the redemption of Israel out of the slavery of Egypt into the glorious liberty of God's people as the everlasting type of redemption out of the slavery of sin into the liberty of the children of God.[1] On this account Jesus said on earth, "If the Son therefore shall make you free, ye shall be free indeed." And the Scriptures teach us to

---

[1]Ex. 1:14; 4:23; 6:5; 20:2; Deut. 24:18

194

stand fast in the freedom with which Christ made us free. Insight into the freedom opens up to us one of the greatest glories of the life that the grace of God has prepared for us.[2]

In the three passages from the Epistle to the Romans in which sanctification is dealt with, a threefold freedom is spoken of. There is freedom from sin in the sixth chapter, freedom from the law in the seventh, freedom from the law of sin in the eighth.

There is *freedom from sin* (Rom. 6:7, 18, 22). Sin is represented as a power that rules over man under which he is brought and taken captive and that urges him as a slave to evil.[3] By the death of Christ and in Christ, the believer, who is one with Him, is made entirely free from the dominion of sin; it has no more power over him. If, then, he still does sin, it is because he, not knowing his freedom by faith, permits sin still to rule over him. But if by faith he fully accepts what the Word of God thus confirms, then sin has no power over him. He overcomes it by the faith that he is made free from it.[4]

Then there is *freedom from the law*. This leads us deeper into the life of grace than freedom from sin. According to Scripture, law and sin always go together. "The strength of sin is the law." The law does nothing but make the offense greater.[5] The law expresses our sinfulness and cannot help us against sin; but with its demand for perfect obedience, it gives us over hopelessly to the power of sin.

The Christian who does not discern that he is made free from the law will always abide under sin.[6] Christ and the law cannot rule over us together; in every endeavor to fulfill the law as believers, we are taken captive by sin.[7] The Christian must know that he is entirely free from the law, from the "you must" that stands without us and over us; then for

---

[2]John 8:32, 36; Gal. 4:21, 31; 5:1
[3]John 8:34; Rom. 7:14, 23; 2 Pet. 2:19
[4]Rom. 5:21; 6:13, 14
[5]Rom. 4:15; 5:13, 20; 7:13; 1 Cor. 15:56
[6]Rom. 6:15; 7:5
[7]Rom. 7:5, 23

the first time shall he know what it is to be free from sin.

Then there is also *freedom from the law of sin*—actual liberation from the power of sin in our members. What we have in Christ—freedom from sin and from the law—is inwardly appropriated for us by the Spirit of God. "The law of the Spirit of life in Christ Jesus hath made me free from the law of sin and death." The Holy Spirit in us takes the place of the law over us. "If ye are led of the Spirit, ye are not under the law." Freeing from the law is not anything external but takes place according to the measure the Spirit obtains dominion in us and leads us. "Where the Spirit of the Lord is, there is liberty." As the law of the Spirit rules in us, we are made free from the law of sin. We are then free to serve God.[8]

"Free" expresses a condition in which nothing hinders me from being what I would be and ought to be. In other words, to be free is to be able to do what I would. The power of sin over us, the power of the law against us, the power of the law of sin in us hinder us. But he that stands in the freedom of the Holy Spirit—he that is truly free—nothing can prevent or hinder him from being what he would be and ought to be. As it is the nature of a tree to grow upwards, and it also grows as it is free from all hindrances, so a child of God then grows to what he ought to be and shall be. And according as the Holy Spirit leads him into this freedom, there springs up the joyful consciousness of his strength for the life of faith. He joyfully shouts, "I can do all things through Christ that strengtheneth me." "Thanks be unto God which always leadeth us in triumph in Christ."

Son of God, anointed with the Spirit to announce freedom to the captives, make me also truly free. Let the Spirit of life in you, my Lord, make me free from the law of sin and of death. I am your ransomed one. Oh, let me live as your freed one, who is hindered by nothing from serving you. Amen.

---

[8]2 Cor. 3:17; Gal. 5:18

1. The freedom of the Christian extends over his whole life. He is free in relation to the institutions and teachings of men. "Ye were bought with a price: become not bond-servants of men" (1 Cor. 7:23; Col. 2:20). He is free in relation to the world and in the use of what God gives; he has power to possess it or to dispense with it, to enjoy it or to sacrifice it (1 Cor. 8:8; 9:4, 5).

2. This freedom is no lawlessness. We are free from sin and the law to serve God in the Spirit. We are not under the law, but we give ourselves, with free choice and in love, to Him who loved us (Rom. 6:18; Gal. 5:13; 1 Pet. 2:16). Not under the law but also not without law. We are in the law—a new, a higher law, "the law of the Spirit of life," "the law of liberty," "the law written in [our] hearts," which is our rule and measure (Rom. 8:2; James 1:25; Rom. 2:15). In this last passage the translation ought to be: "bound by a law to Christ."

3. This freedom has its subsistence from the Word and also in it: the more the Word abides in me and the truth lives in me, the freer I become (John 8:31, 32, 36).

4. Freedom manifests itself in love. I am free from the law, and from men, and from institutions, to be able now like Christ to surrender myself for others (Rom. 14:13, 21; Gal. 5:13; 6:1).

5. This glorious liberty to serve God and our neighbor in love is a spiritual thing. We cannot by any means seize it and draw it to us. It becomes known only by a life in the Holy Spirit. "Where the Spirit of the Lord is, there is liberty." "If ye are led by the Spirit, ye are not under the law." It is the Holy Spirit who makes free. Let us allow ourselves to be introduced by Him into the glorious liberty of the children of God. "The Spirit of life in Christ Jesus hath made me free from the law of sin and death."

CHAPTER 50

Growth

"So is the kingdom of God, as if a man should cast seed into the ground; and should sleep and rise night and day, and the seed should spring and grow up, he knoweth not how. For the earth bringeth forth fruit of herself; first the blade, then the ear, after that the full corn in the ear" (Mark 4:26–28).

"The Head, from which all the body . . . increaseth with the increase of God" (Col. 2:19).

"[That we] may grow up into him, in all things which is the head, even Christ: from whom the whole body . . . maketh increase" (Eph. 4:15, 16).

Death is always a standing still, life is always movement, progressiveness. Increase or growth is the law of all created life; consequently, the new life in man is destined to increase, and always by becoming stronger. As there are in the seed and in the earth a life and power of growth by which the plant is impelled to have its full height and fruit, so there is in the seed of eternal life an impelling force by which also that life always increases and grows with a divine growth until we come to a perfect man—to the measure of the stature of the fullness of Christ.[1]

In this parable of the seed that springs up of itself and becomes great and bears fruit, the Lord teaches us two of the most important lessons on the growth of the spiritual life.

---

[1]Eph. 4:13; 2 Thess. 1:3, 4

The one is that of its *self-sufficiency* and the other that of its *gradualness*.

The first lesson of self-sufficiency is for those who ask what they are to do in order to grow and advance more in grace. As the Lord said of the body, "Which of you by being anxious can add one cubit unto his stature? Consider the lilies of the field how they grow"; so He says to us here that we can do nothing, and need do nothing, to make the spiritual life grow.[2] Do you not see how, while man slept, the seed sprang up and became high (he knew not how) and how the earth brought forth fruit of itself? When man has once sowed, he must depend upon God to care for the growth. He has not to care; he must trust and rest.

And must man then do nothing? He can do nothing. It is from within that the power of life must come—from the life, from the Spirit, implanted in him. To the growth itself he can contribute nothing; it shall be given to him to grow.[3]

All that he can do is to let the life grow. All that can hinder the life, he must take away and keep away. If there are thorns and thistles that take away place and power in the soil which the plant must have, he can take them away.[4] The plant must have its place in the earth alone and undivided. For this the husbandman can care; then it grows further *of itself*. So must the Christian take away what can hinder the growth of the new life. He must surrender the heart entire and undivided for the new life, to hold it alone in possession and to fill it, so that it may grow free and unhindered.[5]

The husbandman can also provide what the plant requires in the way of food or drink; he can fertilize and moisten the soil as it may be needful. So must the believer see that the new life provided nourishment out of the Word, the living water of the Spirit, by prayer. It is in Christ that the

[2]Hos. 14:5; Matt. 6:25, 27, 30
[3]Ps. 92:12, 13; Gal. 2:20; Col. 3:3
[4]Matt. 13:22, 23; John 15:1, 2
[5]Song of Sol. 2:15; Heb. 12:1

new life is planted; from Him it increases with divine growth. Abide rooted in Him by the exercise of faith; the life will grow of itself.[6] Give it what it must have; take away what can hinder it. The life will grow and increase of itself.

The second lesson of the parable is the gradualness of the growth: "first the blade, then the ear, after that the full corn in the ear." Do not expect everything at once. Give God time. By faith and endurance we inherit the promise—the faith that knows that it has everything in Christ; the endurance that expects everything in its time according to the rule and the order of the divine government. Give God time. Give the new life time. It is by continued abiding in the earth that the plant grows; it is by continuous standing in grace, in Christ in whom God has planted us, that the new life grows.[7]

Yes, give the new life sufficient time—time in prayer; time in fellowship with God; time in continuous exercise of faith; time in persistent separation from the world. Give it time. Slow but sure, hidden but real, in apparent weakness but with heavenly power, the divine growth will bring forth the perfect man in Christ.

Lord God, graciously strengthen the faith of your children that their growth and progress are in your hands. Enable them to see what a precious, powerful life was implanted in them by yourself, a life that grows with a divine growth. Enable them by faith and patience to inherit the promises. And teach them in that faith to take away all that can hinder the new life to bring forward all that can further it, so that you may make your work in them glorious. Amen.

1. For a plant, the principal supplier is the sun in which it stands and out of which it draws its strength. For the Christian, this also is the principal thing: he is in Christ. Christ is all. He must grow up in Him, for out of Him the

---

[6]John 15:4, 5; Col. 2:6, 7
[7]Heb. 3:13; 6:12, 15; James 5:7

body obtains its increase. To abide in Christ by faith—that is the main thing.

2. Remember that faith must set itself toward a silent restfulness, that growth is just like that of the lilies in God's hands, and that He will see that we increase and grow strong.

3. By this firm and joyful faith, we become "strengthened with all power according to the might of his glory, unto all patience and longsuffering with joy" (Col. 1:11).

4. This faith—that God cares for our growth—takes away all anxiety and gives courage for doing the two things that we have to do: the taking away of what may be obstructive to the new life, the bringing forward of what may be serviceable to it.

5. Observe well the distinction between planting and growing. Planting is the work of a moment—in a moment the earth receives the seed; after that comes the slow growth. Without delay—immediately—the sinner must receive the word; before conversion there is no delay. Then with time follows the growth of the seed.

6. The main thing is Christ; from Him and in Him is our growth. He is the soil that of itself brings forth fruit—we know not how. Hold daily communion with Him.

CHAPTER 51

Searching the Scriptures

"O how love I thy law: it is my meditation all the day" (Ps. 119:97).

"Search the scriptures. . . . They are they which testify of me" (John 5:39).

"The word . . . did not profit them, not being mixed with faith in them that heard" (Heb. 4:2).

At the beginning of this book there is more than one passage on the use of God's Word in the life of grace. I would once again come back to this all-important point. I cannot too earnestly and urgently address this call to new believers: Upon your use of the Word of God, your spiritual life in great measure depends. Man lives by the word that proceedeth from the mouth of God. Therefore seek with your whole heart to learn how to use God's Word properly. To this end, receive the following suggestions.

Read the Word *more with the heart than with the understanding*. With the understanding I would know and comprehend; with the heart I desire, and love, and hold fast. Let the understanding be the servant of the heart. Beware of the understanding of the carnal nature that cannot receive spiritual things.[1] Deny your understanding and wait in humility on the Spirit of God. On every occasion, keep silent in your reading of the Word, and say to yourselves: "This word I now

---

[1] 1 Cor. 1:21, 27; 2:6, 12, 14; Col. 2:18, 23

receive in my heart, to love and to let it live in me."[2]

Read the Word always *in fellowship with the living God*. The power of a word depends on my conviction regarding the man from whom it comes. First set yourself in loving fellowship with the living God under the impression of His nearness and love. Deal with the Word under the full conviction that He, the eternal God, is speaking with you; and let the heart be silent to listen to God, to God himself.[3] Then the Word certainly becomes to you a great blessing.

Read the Word *as a living Word in which the Spirit of God dwells and that certainly works in those that believe*. The Word is seed. Seed has life and grows and yields fruit of itself. The Word has life, and of itself grows and yields fruit.[4] If you do not fully understand it, if you do not feel its power, carry it in your heart; meditate upon it. It will of itself begin to yield a working and growth in you.[5] The Spirit of God is with and in the Word.

Read it *with the conviction to be not only a hearer but a doer of the Word*. Let the great question be: What would God have me do with this word? If the answer is, He would have me believe it and depend upon Him to fulfill it, do this immediately from the heart. If the word is a command of what you are to do, yield yourself immediately to do it.[6] Oh, there is an unspeakable blessedness in the doing of God's Word and in the surrender of myself to be and to act just as the Word says and would have it. Be not hearers but doers of the Word.

Read the Word *with time*. I see more and more that one obtains nothing on earth without time. Give the Word time. Give the Word time to come into your heart at every occasion on which you sit down to read it. Give it time, in the persistence with which you hold to it from day to day and month

---

[2]Ps. 119:10, 11, 47; Rom. 10:8; James 1:21

[3]Gen. 17:3; 1 Sam. 3:9, 10; Isa. 50:4; 52:6; Jer. 1:2

[4]Mark 4:26, 27, 28; John 6:63; 1 Thess. 2:13; 1 Pet. 1:23

[5]Ps. 119:15, 40, 48, 69; 2 Tim. 3:16, 17

[6]Matt. 5:19, 20; 7:21, 24; Luke 11:28; James 1:21, 25

after month.[7] By perseverance you become exercised and more accustomed to the Word; the Word begins to work. Do not be discouraged when you do not understand the Word. Hold on, take courage, give the Word time. Later on the Word will explain itself. David had to meditate day and night to understand it.

Read the Word *with a searching of the Scriptures*. The best explanation of the Bible is the Bible itself. Take three or four texts upon a point; set them close to one another and compare them. See wherein they agree and wherein they differ; where they say the same thing or again something else. Let the Word of God at one time be cleared up and confirmed by what He said at another time on the same subject. This is the safest and the best explanation. Even the sacred writers use this method of instruction with the Scriptures: *"and again."*[8] Do not complain that this method takes too much time and effort. It is worthy of the pains; your efforts will be rewarded. On earth you have nothing without pains.[9] Even the bread of life we have to eat in the sweat of our face. He that would go to heaven never goes without taking pains. Search the Scriptures; it will be richly recompensed to you.

New believer, let one of my last and most earnest words to you be this: on your dealing with the Word of God depends your growth, your power, your life. Love God's Word then; esteem it sweeter than honey, better than thousands of gold or silver. In the Word God can and will reveal His heart to you. In the Word Jesus will communicate himself and all His grace. In the Word the Holy Spirit will come to renew your heart and all your thoughts according to the mind and will of God. Oh, then, read not simply enough of the Word to keep you from backsliding, but reckon it one of your chief occupations on earth to yield yourself that God may fill you with His Word, that He may fulfill His Word in you.

---

[7]Deut. 6:5–9; Ps. 1:2; 119:97; Jer. 15:16

[8]Isa. 34:16; John 19:37; Acts 17:11; Heb. 2:13

[9]Prov. 2:4, 5; 3:13, 18; Matt. 13:44

Lord God, what grace it is that you have spoken to us in your Word, that we in your Word have access to your heart, to your will, to your love. Oh, forgive us our sins against your precious Word. And, Lord, let the new life become so strong by the Spirit in us that all its desire shall be to abide in your Word. Amen.

In the middle of the Bible stands Psalm 119, in which the praise and the love of God's Word are so strikingly expressed. It is not enough for us to read through the divisions of this psalm successively; we must take its principal points and one with another seek what is said in different passages upon each of these. Let us, for example, take the following points, observing the indications of the answers, and seek in this way to come under the full impression of what is taught of the glory of God's Word:

1. The blessing that the Word gives (vv. 1, 2, 6, 9, 11, 14, 24, 45, 46, 47, etc.).

2. The designations that in this psalm are given to God's Word.

3. How we have to handle the Word (observe, walk, keep, mark, etc.)

4. Prayer for divine teaching (vv. 5, 10, 12, 18, 19, 26).

5. Surrender to obedience to the Word (vv. 93, 105, 106, 112, 128, 133).

6. God's Word the basis of our prayer (vv. 41, 49, 58, 76, 107, 116, 170).

7. Observance as the ground of confidence in prayer (vv. 77, 159, 176).

8. Observance as promised upon the hearing of prayer (vv. 8, 17, 33, 34, 44).

9. The power to observe the Word (vv. 32, 36, 41, 42, 117, 135, 146).

10. The praise of God's Word (vv. 54, 72, 97, 129, 130, 144).

11. The confident confession of obedience (vv. 102, 110, 121, 168).

12. Personal communion with God, seen in the use of *Thou* and *I*, *Thine* and *mine*.

I have mentioned merely a few points and a few verses. Seek out more and mark them until your mind is filled with the thoughts about the Word, which the Spirit of God desires to give you.

Read with great thoughtfulness the words of that man of faith, George Müller: "The power of our spiritual life will be according to the measure of the room that the Word of God takes up in our life and in our thoughts. After an experience of fifty-four years, I can solemnly declare this. For three years after my conversion I used the Word little. Since that time I searched it with diligence, and the blessing was wonderful. From that time, I have read the Bible through a hundred times in order, and at every time with increasing joy. Whenever I start afresh with it, it appears to me as a new book. I cannot express how great the blessing is of faithful, daily, regular searching of the Bible. The day is lost for me on which I have used no rounded time for enjoying the Word of God.

"Friends sometimes say: 'I have so much to do that I can find no time for regular Bible study.' I believe that there are few that have to work harder than I have. Yet it remains a rule with me never to begin my work until I have had sweet fellowship with God. After that I give myself heartily to the business of the day—that is, to God's work, with only intervals of some minutes for prayer."

CHAPTER 52

The Lord the Perfecter

"I will cry unto God most high; unto God that performeth all things for me" (Ps. 57:2).

"The Lord will perfect that which concerneth me" (Ps. 138:8).

"Being confident of this very thing, that he which hath begun a good work in you will perform it until the day of Jesus Christ" (Phil. 1:6).

"For of him, and through him, and to him, are all things: to whom be glory for ever" (Rom. 11:36).

We read that David was once discouraged by unbelief and said, "I shall one day perish by the hand of Saul." So even the Christian may fear that he shall one day perish. This is because he looks at himself and what is in him, and does not set his trust wholly upon God. It is because he does not yet know God as the perfecter. He does not yet know what is meant by His name, "I am Alpha and Omega, the beginning and the ending . . . the first and the last." If I really believe in God as the beginning, then I must also trust Him as the continuation.

God is the beginning: "He who began a good work in you"; "Ye have not chosen me, but I have chosen you." It is because of God's free choice from before the foundation of the world that we have become believers and have the new life.[1] Those who are still unconverted have not entered into this election; for them there is the offer of grace and the summons to surrender. Those

---

[1]John 15:16; Rom. 8:29, 30; Eph. 1:4, 11

who enter in find the full blessing of being the beloved of God.

It is of great importance to hold fast this truth: He has begun the good work. Then shall every thought of God strengthen the confidence that He will also perfect it. His faithfulness, His love, His power are all pledged that He will perfect the good work that He began. Read how God has taken more than one oath regarding His unchangeable faithfulness; your soul will rest in this and find courage.[2]

And how shall He finish His work? That which has its origin *from* Him is sustained *by* Him and shall one day be brought *to* Him and His glory. There is nothing in your life, temporal or spiritual, for which the Father will not care, because it has influence upon you for eternity.[3]

There is no moment of day or night in which the silent growth of your soul is not to go forward; the Father will take care of this if you believe. There is no part of your destiny as a child of God, perhaps in things of which you have as yet not the least thought, but the Father will continue and complete His work in it.[4] However, it is upon one condition: You must trust Him for this. You must in faith allow Him to work. You must trustfully say, "The Lord will perfect that which concerneth me." You must trustfully pray, "I will cry unto God that performeth all things for me." Christian, let your soul become full of the thought that the whole care—the continuation and the perfecting of God's work in you—is in His hands.[5]

And how glorious shall the perfecting be! In our spiritual life, God is prepared to exhibit His power in making us partakers of His holiness and the image of His Son. He will equip and establish us in a condition for all the blessed work in His kingdom that He would have from us. Our body He will make like the glorious body of His Son. We may wait for the coming of the Son from heaven to take His own to Him. He will unite us in one body with all His chosen and will receive and make us dwell

---

[2]Gen. 28:15; Ps. 89:29, 34–36; Isa. 54:9, 10; Jer. 33:25, 26

[3]Matt. 6:25, 34; 1 Pet. 5:7

[4]Isa. 27:2, 3; 51:12, 13

[5]Heb. 10:35; 13:5, 6, 20, 21; 1 Pet. 5:10

forever in His glory. Oh, how can we think that God will not perfect His work? He will surely do it, He will gloriously do it, for everyone that trusts Him for it.

New believer, say in deep assurance of faith, "The Lord will perfect that which concerneth me." In every need say continually with great boldness, "I will call upon God, who performeth all things for me." And let the song of your life be the joyful doxology, "From him, and through him, and to him are all things; to him be the glory for ever." Amen.

Lord God, who shall perfect that which concerneth me, teach me to know you and to trust you. And let every thought of the new life go hand in hand with the joyful assurance that He who began a good work in me will perfect it. Amen.

1. "He that endureth to the end, the same shall be saved." It brings but little profit to begin well; we must hold the beginning of our hope firm unto the end (Matt. 10:27; 24:13; Heb. 3:14, 16; 11:12).

2. How do I know whether I am partaker of the new birth? "As many as are led by the Spirit of God, they are the sons of God" (Rom. 8:14). The faith that God has received me is matured, is confirmed, by works, by a walk under the leading of the Spirit.

3. How can anyone know for certain that he will persevere unto the end? By faith in God the perfecter. We may take the Almighty God as our keeper. He who gives himself in sincerity to Him and trusts wholly in Him to perfect His work obtains a divine certainty that the Lord has him and will hold him fast unto the end.

Child of God, live in fellowship with your Father; live the life of faith in your Jesus with an undivided heart, and all fear of falling away shall be taken away from you. The living sealing of the Holy Spirit shall be your assurance of perseverance unto the end.